THE
SENIOR
CITIZENS'
HANDBOOK

A nuts and bolts approach to more comfortable living

BY WESLEY J. SMITH

PRICE STERN SLOAN
Los Angeles

For Mom, who proves that the golden years
can be a youthful experience.

Copyright © 1989 by Wesley J. Smith
Published by Price Stern Sloan, Inc.
360 North La Cienega Boulevard, Los Angeles, California 90048

ISBN: 0-89586-795-8

10 9 8 7 6 5 4 3 2 1
First Printing

Library of Congress Cataloging-in-Publication Data

Smith, Wesley J.
    The Senior Citizens' Handbook : A Nuts and Bolts Guide to Senior
Living / by Wesley J. Smith.

    p.   cm.
  ISBN 0-89586-795-8
  1. Aged—United States—Life skills guides.   2. Aged—Services
for—United States.   3. Retirement—United States.   4. Estate
planning—United States.   I. Title.
HQ1064.U5S593   1989   88-39744
646.7'9'0973—dc19   CIP

TABLE OF CONTENTS

PREFACE

The seed which grew into this book was planted in the spring of 1987 when I received a call from a dear woman named Frances Katz who had read my first book, *The Lawyer Book*, and called to express her appreciation. She made a comment that she was to repeat often as our friendship grew. "Wesley," she said, "I'm over seventy and I want you to write a book that will tell me how to be old."

At first I demurred. How can anyone tell anyone else how to "be" anything? I thanked Frances for her kind words and suggestions, I went on to write *The Doctor Book*. Yet, Frances persisted. She had planted a seed and by golly, she was going to see it grow. And grow it did.

As a frequent talk show guest, I began to notice an enormous interest on the part of the audiences in estate planning. "Living Trusts" especially would always generate a blizzard of telephone response. So would topics concerning Medicare, nursing homes, housing and anything else related to what I shall call "senior services."

I also came to realize that the subject is very relevant to me. My beautiful mother is 71 (going on 30) and I want to make sure that she receives all of the benefits that her years entitle her to. Besides, I am a "baby boomer" myself and the word gray is beginning to take on a whole new meaning.

This prompted me to write a book that would benefit not only seniors but also their loved ones and caregivers. I wanted to clarify some of the issues that concern senior citizens and to assemble under one roof the wide range of services available to make their life more livable.

And that's the key word for us all no matter what stage of life we find ourselves in. My great hope for this book is that it will help seniors and their loved ones live better and get the most joy and fulfillment out of life. After all, that is what this whole ball game is all about.

—Wesley J. Smith

ACKNOWLEDGMENTS

This book could not have been written without the cooperation of the following persons and organizations:

Helen L. Abbott; Charles Alpert Atty. at Law; U.S. Representative Anthony Bielenson and Staff; Pastor John Barnett; Judy Belamy; Theresa Chavez, M.S.W.; Deborah Cherry, PhD.; Barbara Cook; John P. Coyle, M.S.W.; James W. Davis, Jr., M.D.; Angela Edwards; Daniel V. Ehrensaft, M.D.; John Fenton; Michael B. Kamiel, M.D., F.R.C.P., F.A.C.P.; Stephen Kozel, Phar.D.; Viola Langman; Patricia Charles LaRose; Roger Lawson; Marie Liston, M.S.W.; Altheia Ludowitz; Elizabeth Mandehr; Wendy Morris; Stephanie Multer Goor; Nathan Murillo, PhD.; Ralph Nader; Detective George A. Nielsen; U.S. Representative Claude Pepper and Staff; Jack A. Rameson III, Atty. at Law; Ann Sagrin; Toby Scott; Dean Shetler; Garrett E. Snipes, M.D., F.A.A.F.P.; Mark Spencer; Paul Steinmetz, M.A., M.F.C.C.; George K. Takahashi; Nancy Tamarisk, R.N.; Ron Tamarisk, R.N.; Laura Terry; Donna F. ver Steeg, R.N., PhD., F.A.A.N.; Nancy Wexler, M.F.C.C.; David I. Zeitlin.

ACTION; American Association of Retired Persons; American Board of Internal Medicine; American Cancer Society; American Diabetes Association; American Heart Association; American Medical Association; Arizona Energy and Older Adult Network; Arkay Travel & Tours; Attorneys Association; Bank of America; Brotman Medical Center; California Association of Homes for the Aging; California Lutheran Home; California State Hospice Association; Consumers Union; Department of Human Resources; Department of Public Social Services of Los Angeles County; Economic Crime Project National District; Elderhostel; Forest Lawn Mortuaries; Gerontology Associates; Grace Community Church; Gray Panthers; H.I.P.; Health Insurance Associates of America; Huntington Memorial Hospital; Jobs Club; Lifeline; Long Securities Corporation; Los Angeles Council on Careers for Older Americans; Los Angeles Police Department, Bunco/

Forgery Division; McGeorge School of Law Victims of Crime Resource Center; Medic Alert Foundation; National Arthritis Foundation; National Association of Private Geriatric Care Managers; National Center For Home Equity Conversion; National Funeral Directors Association; National Hospice Organization; National Institute on Aging; National Organization for Victim Assistance; National Senior Citizens Law Center; The Nolo Press; Office of Attorney General for the State of California; Older Women's League; City of Phoenix Department of Human Resources; R.S.V.P., Retired Seniors Volunteer Program; Senior Companion Program; Seniors Abroad; St. Johns Medical Center, Sun City; The Neptune Society; The Travelers Companies; The Visiting Nurse Foundation; U.C.L.A. Gerontology Center; U.C.L.A. Medical Center; U.S. Department of Health and Human Services; U.S. Department of Housing and Urban Development; U.S. House of Representatives Select Committee on Aging; U.S. Peace Corps; U.S. Securities and Exchange Commission; U.S. Postal Service; United Way; Veterans Administration; Wilkinson Multi-Purpose Senior Center.

And finally, allow me to thank those friends, loved ones, and associates whose positive reinforcement, including the occasional kick in the seat, is so deeply appreciated:

My mother, Leona Smith, my grandmother, Gladys Yarborough, Jennie Frankle, Davy Frankle, Dick and Shirley Willey, John Albert, Linda Day, Beverly Golden, Guy Stockwell, Carla Mancari, Gina Francis, Shirley Strick, Frances Katz, Lisa Marsoli, Mary Kirby, Nick Clemente, Leonard Stern, Ron Gold, Gloria Blackman, and everyone at Price Stern Sloan, and the one and only Terrie Frankle-Smith, my wonderful wife.

INTRODUCTION

Wesley J. Smith, the author of this lively and informative book, has proven that knowing enough to ask the right questions can help make life happier and more fulfilling, particularly for older people. Today there are so many opportunities for maintaining health, improving one's mind and contributing to society that a book like Mr. Smith's is most valuable not only to senior citizens, but to the community in general.

Reading through THE SENIOR CITIZENS' HANDBOOK, I was struck by the complexities of modern life. How, I wondered, would a seventy-five year old of the 1830s react to all the advice given in these pages? The 19th century was a far simpler time than our own. The medical knowledge and human interactions that make this book such a necessary companion for our times did not exist then. At that time, there were no professional grief therapists, financial advisers or extensive health and home care services available to the public.

Today there are so many organizations and government programs designed to enrich and improve everyone's life that you owe it to yourself and your family to keep abreast of this information. That's why a comprehensive reference book like THE SENIOR CITIZENS' HANDBOOK can be so important in assisting you to make the most out of this special time in your life. This book offers excellent guidelines for staying healthy, establishing financial security, getting the most for your dollar and contributing actively to your community and country. These are priorities that most people regard as integral to an enjoyable life for themselves and their loved ones.

Wesley Smith writes as if he were conversing with you. A highly trained general practice lawyer, he delivers a great deal of information with clarity and precision. He anticipates your questions and tells you enough to guide your decisions without overwhelming you with complex detail. If you wish to delve deeper into a particular subject, he's right there, directing you to further sources and giving you suggestions on how best to use them.

THE SENIOR CITIZENS' HANDBOOK is a first-rate reference volume that manages to interview you quietly as you go through the book. You'll find yourself responding to these pages with questions like, "Yes, I can become interested in this volunteer program," or "Why am I paying for some medigap insurance policy that is very largely a fraud?" or "For heaven's sake, by making just one phone call to my banker, I can increase my savings income every month," or "Gee, I've got to tell my friend about this service. It's just what she needs."

Looking at this book as a whole, I found the term 'a nuts and bolts guide' to be a most appropriate description. With the number of business, government and nonprofit organizations specifically geared to servicing and selling to older citizens, a reliable and comprehensive guide is exactly what is called for to help today's older consumer through this maze. Too many of these people are exploited by companies that deliberately target them for fraudulent business propositions. So many of these heartbreaking scams can be avoided by simply recognizing the danger signs. Wesley Smith devotes a whole chapter to the most common con games and scams as well as a list of agencies to contact if you do become the victim of fraud.

On a more positive note, there are a number of volunteer groups, nonprofit organizations and various associations that offer all kinds of service and opportunities to older people. THE SENIOR CITIZENS' HANDBOOK includes a generous listing of these as well as their publications. There is so much disinformation about aging that often society gets a distorted view of what it means to be an older person in today's world. I found especially enlightening the medical findings of the National Institute on Aging that dispel the myths about various incapacities being connected to age per se. These myths have been very detrimental to the self-image of older people and their families, and it is gratifying to see they are unfounded. Far too often, this negative stereotyping has led to self-fulfilling prophecies that have been very damaging to the dignity of senior citizens.

Another bonus to readers is the inclusion of recent legislated programs for the elderly. Many of the most useful benefits and rights available to senior citizens go unused because people are unaware that they exist. This guide brings you aboard this ship of untapped wealth and tells you how to go about reaping these often free benefits.

Older citizens are a major human resource of experience, wisdom and promise. They have a great deal to offer society and should not wait for others to ask for their help. With the enormity of problems in our society, we can't afford to have talented people spending their time unhappily uninvolved. After retirement, people have more freedom to speak out; they no longer have to worry about how their opinion may affect their job. They also have more time to apply their creativity and experience to community problems that need their kind insight and compassion.

Wesley Smith's invitation in these brightly written pages is to use knowledge you gain here to become more confident, independent and vital in your personal life and better able to involve yourself in the civic life of your community. This blend of human happiness and productivity ultimately makes your life and that of your community more satisfying and fulfilling. In my mind, Wesley Smith's book is directed at that goal and succeeds admirably.

Ralph Nader
Washington, D.C.

1

Home Sweet Home

Strategies For Retirement Living

Staying In Your Own Home; Owning Vs. Renting; Questions To Ask Yourself When Deciding To Buy; Condominiums And Cooperatives; Mobile Homes; Renting An Apartment; Retirement Communities And Retirement Hotels; Shared Housing; Board And Care; Subsidized Housing.

We all know that one of the necessities of life is adequate housing. It's one thing to have the sun in the morning and the moon at night, but without a roof over our heads, we would have the rain in the morning, mud in the afternoon and bugs at night. Our forefathers and mothers were quick to grasp this fact and thus was born the first housing development, Cave Manor, featuring, well . . . caves. They may not have been pretty, but they were free, assuming you had the strength to evict the resident bear, and they worked. Old and young shared equally in the facilities and humankind survived to create what we call civilization.

As we continued our domination of the planet, our housing patterns changed and grew more complex. From villages we went to hamlets and towns and then to cities. As our population grew, the types of housing diversified, ranging from castles and manor houses for the rich to huts for the poor.

Yet, whatever state of housing each family experienced, the old and young usually lived together under one roof.

And now we've survived into the late twentieth century. Civilization at last! Or is it? Things have changed. The old and young have become "residentially" estranged. Today when the chicks leave the roost, their newly created domiciles no longer have room for Mom and Pop.

Thus was born a whole new industry which we shall call SENIOR HOUSING. And as you'd expect in a "civilized" era, there are more options for succesful seniors than you can shake a lease or mortgage at.

IF IT'S NOT BROKEN, DON'T FIX IT

Just because you've reached retirement age and/or your kids have flown the coop doesn't mean that you have to make a change in your living arrangements. This is true even though you may have lost a little zip off the old fastball, for as we shall see in later chapters, there are an abundance of home services available to those seniors who need a helping hand.

STAYING IN YOUR OWN HOME:

For most of us, our homes are usually our biggest investment and our most valuable asset. This is especially true in later years when a large percentage of seniors own their homes free and clear. But whether you own or rent, here are just a few of the advantages that exist for those who decide that no move is the best move.

Little Or No Mortgage Payments: If you have burned the mortgage or are paying on an older loan, your monthly payments are probably going to be next to nothing by today's standards. Obviously this means more money in your pocket for the important things in life like buying that Harley Davidson "Hog" or Porcshe 924.

Stabilized Rent: For those of you who rent, a good reason for staying put may be a low or stabilized rent. This is especially true in those communities which provide some form of rent control. In such communities rent increases are restricted as long as the tenant doesn't move from the residence. And since many seniors generally have a lower income than they did before retirement, avoiding a raise in the rent may be one of life's priorities.

Maintaining One's Roots: Psychologists tell us that most people do better in life if they feel secure in their surroundings. For senior citizens especially, remaining in a neighborhood where old friends and loved ones live can add greatly to the quality of life. Local ties such as membership in a church or synagogue or club adds to the enjoyment of retirement years. In addition, knowing the lay of the land is a real confidence builder that can make the chores of daily living easier to accomplish. Besides, one of the benefits of growing older should be happy memories, and some memories are best enjoyed in the place where they were created.

Avoiding The Stress Of Moving: Change causes stress, not only for seniors but for everyone. Selling the old homestead and moving to a new neighborhood can cause more stress for an older person than others. After all, it's not easy to break into a new community. It takes time and energy to orient yourself to a new environment, to say nothing of the expense. For many, the expected benefits of a move are just not worth the heartache and inconvenience.

Taking Advantage of Income Opportunities: If you own your home and it has a very high equity (the difference between what is owed and what the property is worth on the open market), you may be able to remain there while cashing in on its value. This can be done by entering into an "Equity Conversion" contract such as a "Reverse Mortgage." (See Chapter 2)

In addition, even if your house is "hocked to the hilt," you can always earn extra money (and obtain some companionship) by renting a room to someone with whom you feel safe and compatible.

STAYING IN YOUR OWN COMMUNITY:

While there are often good reasons for selling your house or moving out of your apartment, it doesn't mean you need to cut all the ties that bind. Before you decide to stay or go, investigate what is available in your community. You may find that you can have the benefits of senior housing as well as the security of staying on familiar ground.

ONWARD AND UPWARD

There's an old saying that goes "the times are changing and you've got to change with the times." This is certainly true when it comes to housing. The home that suited you and your family at one time may be too large or too far removed from services to meet your needs today. You may be having difficulties maintaining your home or perhaps the neighborhood has changed. Maybe your kids live in a different city, and you want to live near them. Whatever your personal reasons, the time may have come to say, "I'm out of here!"

But where to go? There's the rub! No intelligent decision can be made without investigating the options available in the locality where you intend to settle whether it's across the street or in a different time zone. Today there are many options available to seniors who want to make a change.

NOTE: When people think of senior housing, they often think in terms of nursing or convalescent homes. Nothing could be further from the truth. Only a small minority of seniors actually live in nursing homes and both government and private sectors work very hard to keep it that way.

PRIVATE LIVING:

By private living I mean housing options that are no different from those available to the younger members of the community such as houses, apartments and condominiums.

Owning Your Own House: As anyone who has owned their own house will tell you, there are a number of advantages to ownership, among them are:

Freedom. When you own your house, you can do just about anything you want with it (subject to zoning and other regulations). Do you want to paint your bathroom purple? Just pay for the paint. Do you want to pound nails in the walls so you can hang your Heavy Metal Rock Posters up? Any local hardware store will gladly sell you a hammer. Do you want to barbecue in the middle of winter? Charcoal briquettes will probably be on sale. You can do most anything so long as you don't reduce local property values.

Tax Benefits. When you pay your house payment, most of the money paid is interest paid to the mortgage lender. That's the bad news. The good news is that interest paid on a purchase money loan as well as money paid for property tax is tax deductible. Since renters pay those expenses in their rent, you do get a break in taxes by owning rather than renting.

Increased Estate Value. House payments also offer you something more tangible than simply being allowed to occupy the premises for another month. They pay for ownership that increases the value of your estate. Also, property values have a tendency to rise with little or no effort on your part. And these "paper profits" can easily be translated into cold, hard cash.

Stability. When you own your own home, you own more than property. You buy into a neighborhood that will probably remain relatively stable over a long period of time. You buy a mortgage or trust deed payment that will either never change, such as a fixed rate loan, or you get a variable rate loan that will ideally rise or fall slowly over the years. You buy a location where community services and amenities are known and unlikely to change dramatically during the course of your ownership. In other words, you buy a new set of roots that will help nourish you and help you continue to thrive.

Intangibles. Last, but not least, there is something special about saying "my home." There is the sense of owning your own space that no one can take away. Call it satisfaction, call it peace of mind; home ownership is and always will be a large part of the American dream.

Of course, ownership isn't for everyone. Before deciding to buy, ask yourself the following questions:

Do I Want The Responsibility? House ownership brings burdens as well as benefits. Maintenance, for example, is tough enough when you're 35 or 40, but when you're 65 or 70 it can be too burdensome. Also, home ownership can mean a loss of independence. You may find yourself mowing the lawn when you'd rather be playing golf. Or you may be reluctant to travel and leave your home unattended for long periods of time. Remember, your house is going to be a jealous mistress that requires a lot of attention and love.

Can I Afford To Buy? There's more to buying a house than knowing the price and paying the monthly loan payment. First there is the down payment and the closing costs. Maintenance is an ongoing expense and at some point, house repairs will be needed. There are also unexpected costs such as special assessments or storm damage. And don't forget the expense of furnishing a new home. So look before you leap. The financial hole you dig may be deeper than you first expected.

> **NOTE:** If you are thinking of moving to an area known for its balmy weather and good retirement living, check the prices before making any commitments. Housing costs are usually much higher in such locales than they may be where you are living now. A house in California, for example, can cost up to three times that of its equal in states like Kansas or Wisconsin.

Will I Be Hurt By Being Tied Down? One fact of home ownership that is often overlooked is the restriction it places on your mobility. For example, assume you decide that the time has come to sell your home and make some other living arrangements. Even under the best of circumstances, you are probably going to have at least a two-month escrow period, and that's after you accept an offer to buy. If mortgage interest rates high, it may take months to even receive any offers.

Will I Feel Insecure In My Own House? Unless you buy a house located in a senior retirement community that provides security, you will be subject to the same dangers of burglary and vandalism as anyone else in the neighborhood. If this prospect upsets you or if security in the physical sense is one of the top items on your housing agenda, independent home ownership may not be for you.

Owning a Condominium or Cooperative: For many seniors, the condo or co-op is a happy medium between owning a house and renting an apartment. A condominium is a unit in an apartment building where you own your own unit and share the ownership of the common grounds, usually in direct proportion to the size of the unit.

A cooperative building is owned entirely by the co-op itself. When purchasing a unit in the co-op, you are actually buying into the legal organization that owns the facility and your ownership gives you the right to live in a specific unit.

Co-ops and condos offer pros and cons as measured against house ownership.

Benefits: When you own a condominium or co-op, you are relieved of using your own elbow grease for maintenance. Many such facilities offer amenities that might be cost prohibitive in a single residence format such as swimming pool, spa, putting green and other resort amenities. Security is usually good in a condo/co-op environment because you will generally know who your neighbors are. Tax benefits are also similar to those listed under house ownership. Finally, there are usually social advantages including a clubhouse for parties and a friendly sociable atmosphere.

Drawbacks: When you own a condominium or co-op, you do lose some of the freedom you enjoy when owning a house. You are not in control of the look of your property because you are subject to the rules and bylaws of the condominium cooperative or association. These restrictions may not be limited to the look of your home, but may also restrict your right to have grandchildren or other guests stay for extended times on the premises, and the right to keep a pet. You are also subject to monthly charges for maintenance of the common areas such as pool, walkways, snow removal, common utility charges, etc. You may also be subject to special levies for improvements such as a reroofing or installing a new furnace. Most of the decisions concerning the complex as a whole are made by a board of directors elected by the owners, so decisions might be made with which you disagree. It may also be more difficult to sell a condominium or cooperative unit than a single family residence. Many cooperatives restrict the equity (increase in value) you may earn during your time of ownership and, under certain circumstances, may force you to sell your ownership interest. It is always a good idea to hire a lawyer when purchasing a condo or co-op so that you will know what you are buying into.

NOTE: When deciding to buy a condominium, be sure the majority of residents of the facility are owners and not renters. Absentee landlords who control the board of directors may be less willing to spend money for needed improvements and maintenance than owners who live on the premises.

NOTE: Cooperatives may restrict your right to sell to whomever you choose since the board of directors generally has the right to approve or disapprove of your potential buyer.

Owning A Mobile Home: Suppose you don't have the money to buy a house or condo, yet you want the benefits and satisfaction of home ownership. And, you insist upon living in a well maintained adult community where you have independence as well as the security of knowing neighbors and the fun of recreational activities. You can have it all by purchasing a mobile home and having it set up at an adult mobile home community.

I am not talking about the trailer which can be hitched to the old Model A and taken wherever the rubber meets the road. Today's mobile homes are pre-fabricated and can be as large as a small three bedroom house. They're about as mobile as an off-shore oil drilling platform which means you can move them, but you don't want to do it very often. While they can be almost as luxurious as a house or condo, they cost far less, ranging in price from around $18,000 to $45,000 new.

There is an abundance of mobile home parks which cater exclusively to older adults. Many offer amenities such as a swimming pool, spa, clubhouse, golf and/or tennis. Of course, the quality of the facilities varies depending on how much you want to pay per month to rent the space. All parks provide for maintenance of common areas. For many seniors, mobile home parks hit the livability spot.

If you believe mobile home life may be for you, here are some things you should know.

—You must pay for delivery of your home in addition to the purchase price unless you buy one already installed.

—Financing may be harder to obtain or may have higher interest rates than traditional housing. Most mobile homes are financed through retail installment contracts instead of mort-gages or trust deeds.

> **NOTE**: Today you can obtain long-term Veteran's Housing Authority (VHA) and Federal Housing Authority (FHA) loans for the purchase of mobile homes. Contact your nearest federal offices to see if you qualify.

—As with condominiums, you will usually pay two monthly payments: the monthly payment on the purchase loan (assuming you don't pay cash) and the monthly rental fee to the mobile home park.

—If you purchase an older home and wish to move it to a new site, you may run into problems since many mobile home parks will not rent to older units.

—As with condos and co-ops, each park will have different rules regarding important matters such as pets, visiting grandchildren and the right of the landlord to raise the rent. Be sure to read the small print and ask any questions you may have before you sign on the dotted line.

—Some mobile homes contain pressed wood products that use formaldehyde in the binding process. When a mobile home is new, the formaldehyde is emitted in fumes that can cause severe reactions in some people. Discuss your potential sensitivity to formaldehyde with your doctor since some of the symptoms, such as nausea or aggravation of heart disease, can be quite serious.

—Unlike real estate, mobile homes generally experience a significant loss in value once they are purchased. That means you will probably take a loss if you sell your mobile home.

Of course, just because you are buying a mobile home doesn't mean you have to live in a mobile home park. Many seniors place their mobile homes on their own land. If you intend to do so, be sure to check out local zoning laws regarding utility hookup and sewage disposal.

NOTE: When purchasing a mobile home manufactured after 1976, be sure it complies with federal standards. Those homes built in accordance with HUD (Department Of Housing And Urban Development) standards will have a red and silver metal plate attached to the outside.

Renting An Apartment: Do you prefer to avoid the expenses and responsibilities of home ownership? Renting an apartment can be a very liberating experience since there are no lawns to mow or toilets to repair, as those jobs are the landlord's responsibilities. There is usually less space in an apartment than a house so housework takes less time. In short, all you have to do is pay the rent and keep the place clean and the landlord is legally bound to do the rest.

If you intend to rent an apartment, think about these considerations before you start nesting:

How much rent will you be paying and how often can it go up? Unexpected rent increases can throw your life into turmoil. Be sure you understand the terms of your lease before you sign. You should also find out your legal rights and obligations so you can protect yourself in case your landlord forgets the rules.

Decide whether you want to rent under a lease or pay "month to month." A lease is a contract between you and the owner of the apartment granting you the right to live on the premises for a stated period of time at a fixed rental price. A lease protects you from rent increases during the term of the agreement and from eviction, provided that you keep up your end of the bargain. There are also provisions that you must understand before you sign the lease. For example, if you want to move before the lease expires, the landlord can sue you for rent lost due to your breach of the lease term. There will also be a "renewal clause" in your lease contract which allows you to remain in your apartment under the terms of the lease. Sometimes a renewed lease is subject to a rent increase, usually under a financial formula that is stated in the lease itelf. Thus, if you intend to renew, be sure you understand how to do it and the legal consequences of doing so.

> **NOTE**: Leases are usually written by the landlord's lawyers and are filled with legalese which may be as understandable to you as Swahili. Since the terms of the lease are usually drafted in the landlord's favor, it is a very good idea to have your lawyer review the terms of the proposed lease and explain it to you clearly.

Will the landlord properly maintain the property? The best way to find out the answer to this important question is to ask other tenants who live in the building. Be sure to inspect carefully the apartment you are thinking of renting to see whether the sink leaks, the toilet flushes and the garbage disposal works, etc. If any of them do not, be sure to write in the rental agreement that the landlord is obligated to repair them before you move in.

Does the owner of the property live on the premises? If not, does the manager? A "live in" owner/manager can respond to your needs faster than one who only visits when the rent is due. You should always get the name and address of the actual owner so that you have someone to turn to if you are unhappy with the way your apartment is being managed.

If your landlord is not living up to his or her legal obligations, assert yourself. Start by writing a letter that describes in detail the failures and a date by which the matter should be remedied. If that doesn't work, contact your local housing authority or a lawyer to see about applying a little pressure. In some cases you may be able to withhold rent until the landlord takes care of the problem. However, never take such drastic action until you obtain competent legal advise telling you that you have the right to do so and how to do it right.

SENIOR SPECIALS

Much of what we have discussed above is generally applicable to everyone. After all, you don't have to be over the age of 60 to buy a house (just to save up enough money for the down payment). We shall now turn to "opportunities of the housing kind" specifically designed with seniors in mind.

Retirement Communities: When most of us think of housing exclusively designed for seniors, we either think of the nursing home or the retirement community. While nursing homes are primarily populated by older Americans, they are available to patients of any age in need of long-term continuous nursing care. The retirement community, however, has been specifically designed for mature adults from age 50 and up, depending on the rules of the community. (People with young children need not apply except under restricted circumstances.)

Retirement communities can be large, like Sun City, Arizona, which has over sixty thousand residents, or small like a single apartment complex or anything in between. Whatever the size, a retirement community is designed to provide quiet, secure adult living with a defined level of services available to its residents. Resort communities cater to seniors who want to live in the "fast lane" with golf courses, tennis courts, pools, bike paths and big name entertainment offered as incentives to come on board. Retirement hotels offer less glitzy but all basic services such as maid service and meal preparation. All provide an opportunity for peer socializing and interaction.

There are many things to consider when deciding what type of retirement community to join. Here are some of the main issues:

Money. The cost of entering the world of the retirement community will vary from place to place. Some complexes require you to buy your own house or condo that can run well into the six figures. Others cost a modest amount per month. Some charge extra for maintaining common areas and for security. Obviously, the greater the expense, the more you should be getting, so be sure you get a list of the services you are paying for. It is also important to obtain in writing a complete list of charges so that you can compare the communities priced within your budget.

Services. All communities provide a specified level of services. This could range from transportation to stores and doctors' offices to uniformed security to a community room where local residents play bridge. All should have some form of medical assistance available like a hospital or clinic or a resident nurse. Most have a recreation director who can talk with you about ongoing community activities. The important thing to realize is that each community has its own blend of services and activities so don't be afraid to keep looking until you find the perfect fit.

NOTE: Many of the larger retirement communities are so big that a car is a necessity. If this is a problem for you, be sure that there are alternate means of transportation available with schedules that are convenient to your lifestyle.

Locality. The best retirement community in the world may be the worst one for you if it is not located in a place you enjoy. For some, closeness to friends and family will be of primary importance; for others, the absence of snow. For still others, the proximity to major forms of transportation or needed services is key. Whatever your specific needs are, be sure your chosen community meets them.

Ability To Meet Future Needs. Many retirement communities require a minimum level of physical health, not only to join the community, but to stay. It is therefore vital that you obtain the details of the community's policy in writing before you buy or rent. This can be especially important to married couples where one becomes disabled and is forced to leave. Pay close attention to the level of services available should you or your spouse fall into ill health. What kind of adult day care is available? Is there a local senior center or volunteer organization nearby? What about a nursing home? When you select a retirement community, you should plan for the worst and hope for the best. After all, your happy retirement is at stake. If you make the wrong choice you are exposing yourself to moving, one of life's most stressful experiences.

> **NOTE**: Many retirement communities allow you to stay at the facility for a "trial run" at a low fee. If you take advantage of this opportunity, take time away from the fun things and see how the people of the community live. Remember, all that glitters may not be gold.

Continuing Care Communities: There are retirement communities that guarantee care for the rest of your life. These continuing care communities work something like this:

Let's say an older person we'll call Harry is still relatively healthy and active and buys into a continuing care community. Initially Harry leads a relatively independent life on property owned by the community. He participates in community functions and such services as the medical clinic to monitor his blood pressure among other things. If the years take their toll on Harry, he is allowed to move into a part of the community that offers three meals a day and a higher level of care to match his growing needs. His life is made as comfortable as possible. Eventually, he may require nursing home care. Instead of moving away from his home and friends, Harry will be allowed to stay in a long-term nursing facility as long as he needs.

The beauty of continuing care is the security of knowing you won't be forced to leave your home because you are no longer able to care for yourself. You don't have to worry about finding a nursing home since you have already selected one.

Best of all, you can't be kicked out because you can no longer afford to pay for your care since most continuing care communities accept your government benefits when your bank account runs dry.

While these communities can be wonderful, they are not Shangri La, so you need to know the following facts about them before deciding they are for you:

There is a minimum level of health required to apply for entry. For the community to prosper financially the majority of residents must spend at least some time living with a lower level of support services.

> **NOTE**: If you want to live in a continuing care community, be sure to enter before your health turns sour. If you wait too long, you may not be able to get in.

There are multiple levels of care provided depending on the needs of each resident. These levels include:
—independent living, the resident is generally responsible for his or her own care or living unit;
—board and care residents receive meals and some housekeeping services;
—personal care that provides a higher level of personal services such as assisted bathing and grooming;
—convalescent care that provides around-the-clock nursing care and regular doctor visits.

There is a written contract that specifies the rights and responsibilities of the community and the resident; it is called Life Care Contract and it contains many of the following provisions:
—Fees. There is usually a non-refundable application and lump sum entry fee which may or may not be partially refundable in the event of early death or departure from the community. The entry fee is never cheap; it's usually in the middle to high five figure range. In addition, there is a monthly care fee which is adjustable based on the home's projected

expenses. Some communities are doing away with this lump sum entry fee and charging monthly fees based on the level of services received. Others have contracts that require the residents to turn over all of their assets in return for lifetime care. This latter arrangement is becoming less popular.

—Accomodations. Each residence has its own specifications regarding where residents will live. Health and safety are the criteria upon which these decisions are based.

—Services. A typical community will provide most of the following services:

a. three meals a day;

b. basic bed and bath linens on a weekly basis;

c. housekeeping services, usually bi-weekly;

d. maintenance of building and grounds;

e. planned activities designed to meet the physical, social and spiritual needs of the residents;

f. use of general purpose rooms such as a library, community room or chapel;

g. health services (the level of services will vary);

—Medicare. You will be required to participate in Medicare so that the home may be reimbursed for medical services provided under the contract.

—Continuity of care for lifetime residency (except under limited and medically necessary conditions such as if you become a danger to yourself and others).

—The willingness to take your social security payments in return for your care should you run out of money. (This may not be available in every community).

Most communities are non-profit and are affiliated with a religious organization. Although private enterprise is beginning to enter this field, most continuing care homes are non-profit organizations affiliated with religious organizations. Usually, you don't have to be a "believer" to gain entry into the community. Since religious organizations do not actually run the communities, they cannot be held liable should the community go broke.

In choosing a continuing care community, discuss the following with the administration:

Price. Continuing care contracts are expensive. Make sure you can afford the price.

Location. As with retirement communities, the location of the community can mean the difference between existing and really living. Find out if the convalescent facility is located on the same property as the rest of the community. Make sure you will never be far from a spouse, friends or loved ones.

Services. Determine if the services provided will meet your needs whatever your physical condition.

Recreation. What activities does the community sponsor and are they the kind that you enjoy?

Health care. What medical care does the home provide? Do you receive preventive checkups and dental care for the cost of a iving there? Is transportation provided to your own doctor? What health care services are provided in-house?

Cleanliness. Make sure the community is well maintained by inspecting the premises or taking a week's trial run.

Membership in the American Association of Homes For The Aging (AAHA). This affiliation of non-profit homes for the elderly keeps its members professionally certified through quality standards, educational programs and publications aimed at helping the home help you.

The AAHA Continuing Care Accreditation Committee. This accreditation means that the home has met certain minimum standards of quality care.

NOTE: If you are unhappy with your care and cannot get satisfaction from the administrators of the home you live in, contact the AAHA and/or the accreditation committee at the following address:

American Association of Homes
For the Aging
1129 20TH Street NW, Suite 400
Washington D.C. 20036-3489

Potpourri: There are other options for seniors who may not like or cannot afford those listed above. These options include:

Shared Housing. One of the newer concepts in the senior housing block is called shared housing. Two or more seniors rent space in a single family dwelling which is owned by a private or public agency. Each resident has a private room and all share the common spaces such as the kitchen and bathrooms. Rent is usually quite low and can sometimes be waived altogether in return for performing maintenance duties. Many older Americans enjoy the companionship and security of living with others and prefer shared housing.

Board and Care. For those seniors who need assistance in daily living but prefer to avoid a nursing home, board and care residence may be the answer. This type of residence provides daily assistance for a small group of seniors who live together in one home. The money for the care usually comes from social security and/or other benefits that the owners receive in return for providing for the senior's needs.

Subsidized Housing. The federal government through HUD assists seniors in paying their rent either through vouchers or other subsidies. State and local governments also pitch in to help low income seniors. Although help is available, you have to be very poor to qualify.

ECHO Housing. ECHO stands for Elder Cottage Housing Opportunity. These are small cottages installed for temporary sitting on the property of a single family residence. The cottages can be removed when no longer needed. ECHO housing presents a wonderful opportunity for children to have their parents live with them without worrying about having their home take on the ambiance of a two-man submarine. ECHO Housing will be described in more detail in Chapter 10.

Nursing Homes. Nursing homes provide round-the-clock nursing and other medical care and will be discussed in detail in Chapter 10.

> **NOTE**: When choosing your housing option, remember that there are many services such as Meals On Wheels and the Senior Companion Program that can help you live independently. (See Chapters 7 and 10 for more details.)

If you would like more information or assistance in finding suitable housing, contact your local Agency On Aging or your local chapter of the American Association of Retired Persons (AARP), either of which can direct you to the housing resources in your particular area.

2

Putting Bread
On The
Table

Earning Income In The "Golden Years."

The Myths And Facts Of Social Security; How
The Social Security System Operates; The Types
Of Pensions; What To Look Out For In Your Pension Plan; Individual Retirement Accounts; Common Investment Opportunities; Finding Employment In The Senior Years; Equity Home Conversion.

After thirty years of faithful service, the big day had finally
arrived for Philbert E. Pillbody to retire from the old salt mine
as the company's Chief Salt Inspector (Iodized Division). "Just
think," Philbert thought, "I'll finally have the time to write that
book on the great salt shakers of our time!"

Things went very well at first. Philbert wrote the first
chapter of the book he was sure would get him on the Oprah
Winfrey Show where he planned to reveal the truth behind
why the holes in restaurant salt shakers are always plugged up.
"Why didn't I retire ten years ago?" Philbert asked himself.

The answer came in the morning mail. Philbert's variable
rate home mortgage "variabled" up another percentage point.
Worse, his accountant told him that his pension was subject to
income taxes and that the accountant's hourly rate was being
increased by $25 per hour. The bids for the roof repair arrived

as did the letter from Philbert's ex-wife's lawyer . . . but we won't go into that.

"Now, I remember why I didn't retire earlier," Philbert exclaimed, "I needed the money! And it seems I still do."

Like Philbert, many approach retirement hoping to sail through balmy seas only to find themselves in the path of a financial hurricane. Life is expensive and it doesn't become less so because one gets off the treadmill. In fact, even those who are "set" today may find themselves looking for a paycheck tomorrow.

Those who are otherwise secure may choose to go back to work in order to pay for a dream vacation or to buy a new car. There are also many seniors who simply miss the feeling of productivity and self-worth a job brings. Regardless of why one chooses to continue working, the unvarnished truth for many seniors is that finding a reliable source of income is not the same as it used to be.

SOCIAL SECURITY

Mention "income in the golden years" and most people think immediately of social security. It is hard to believe that although it has only been with us for a little over fifty years, social security has become an integral part of American life.

Nonetheless, many of us have only the vaguest notions about how the program really works. As a result, myths have developed that I feel duty bound to debunk.

> MYTH: Social security was designed to guarantee that older Americans will never have to work again once they retire.

> FACT: Social security does not provide enough income for most people to live on. The program was designed to be and continues to function as an income supplement.

MYTH: Once on social security, recipients cannot work or they forfeit all of their benefits.

FACT: Recipients can work and earn a modest amount (approximately $8,200 if 65 or over and $6,000 if younger) without the loss of any benefits. (Ask your local social security office for the current amount). If your earnings exceed the annual exempt amount, you will lose a portion of your benefits; $1 in benefits for every $2 of earnings above the limit ($3 commencing in 1990 if you are at least 65).

MYTH: You must be over 65 to collect social security.

FACT: In order to collect full retirement benefits it is true that you must be 65 (going up to age 67 in gradual increments by the year 2000). However, if you are willing to take reduced benefits, you can start collecting at age 62. A worker can also collect social security if he or she becomes disabled regardless of age, assuming they qualify for the program, as can survivors of deceased workers.

I am omitting any further discussion of disability benefits as they are primarily received by younger workers and their families. If you are a senior citizen and qualify for retirement and disability benefits, you will have to choose the best program for you since you can't collect both. In such case, contact your local social security office for assistance.

MYTH: Social security benefits are not subject to income tax.

FACT: Oh, yes they are. Benefits may be subject to taxes if your earnings plus nontaxable interest income

exceed a certain base amount, currently approximately $25,000 for those age 65 and over. Con-
tact your local social security office for the current
rules or ask your accountant. Once you reach age
70, the I.R.S. can't touch your social security
benefits.

Figuring out social security benefits can be fairly daunting
without the aid of the local office. Nonetheless, I'll give you a
brief rundown on how the system operates.

Qualifying For Social Security: Anyone who's ever earned a
paycheck knows social security is not welfare or a "gift" from
the government. It is something that workers earn through
deductions from their paychecks into the social security system. If you are employed, you and your employer each pay
half the cost, which totals over 14% of your earnings. If you are
self-employed, you pay 100%. No deductions are taken once
your earnings reach a certain level, currently in excess of
$45,000.

Qualifying for the program is relatively easy. You must
earn "work credits" which are measured in "quarters of coverage" that translates into quarters of a year. You earn these
credits by making a minimum amount of money per year. (The
amounts and method of computation vary going back to
1936.) Once you have earned enough work credits, (9 3/4s
years' worth if you reach age 62 in 1990), you qualify for social
security benefits.

The more you earn the more you pay in deductions and
ultimately the more you receive in benefits. There is a ceiling,
however, beyond which even a Donald Trump cannot go. The
exact amount of benefits to which you are entitled will depend
upon what the social security people compute as the average of
your reported income, your age when applying, the type of
benefit you are seeking and the "secret formula" used to compute your benefit. There are two formulas, one beginning in

1936 and the other 1951. They're not really secret, but they are so complicated they may as well be.

> **NOTE**: If you are thinking of applying for social security in the near future and want to find out your prospective benefits, ask your local social security office for a form called Request For Social Security Statement Of Earnings. Fill out the form and return it. Once you have received their response you can ask them to figure out your prospective benefits before you apply.
>
> If social security makes an error in computation of your earnings, it can usually be corrected if it was within the last three years, three months and fifteen days. It's a good idea to request a statement of earnings every few years even if you are not ready to apply for benefits.

Applying For Retirement Benefits: If you qualify for social security, you can apply for your retirement benefits once you have reached the age of 62. However, your benefits will be reduced by about 20% of what you would have received at age 65. This reduction is permanent. If you apply for benefits at age 63 or 64, the penalty is less severe. Conversely, if you apply for benefits after age 65, your benefits increase from a current level of three percent per year over the age of 65 to eight percent per year in 2008. These increases cease at age 70, so there is no reason to delay seeking benefits after that, even if the benefits are taxed.

You should apply approximately three months before you want the benefits to commence. If you apply before age 65, be sure you apply in a timely fashion since you will not be paid any monthly checks lost due to late application. After age 65 you can be repaid for up to six months for checks lost due to late application. When applying for retirement benefits, you should bring the following items with you to your local social security office:

—Your social security card or a record of your number. If you are making a claim based on another person's records, you will need that person's number;

—Proof of your age, usually a birth certificate or baptismal record;

—Your marriage certificate if you are applying for widowed person's benefits (see below);

—Your Form W-2 or a copy of your last federal income tax return if you are self-employed. You will need this to receive an accurate benefit since social security does not have up-to-the-minute records.

—Proof of military service, if any, since being in the military may bring extra work credits.

> **NOTE**: About six months before you reach the age of 62, ask your social security office to compute your expected benefits for ages 62 through age 70. Then compute your other expected sources of income, your anticipated expenses and the intangibles such as your health, retirement plans (and how much you hate your job) and make the decision that's right for you.

Applying For Other Benefits: Social security pays a number of benefits germane to seniors and their families. Here's a short summary:

Dependents Benefits. If you are the spouse of a worker 62 or older who qualifies for disability or retirement benefits, you may receive a supplemental benefit. Spouses under the age of 62 may also receive benefits if they are caring for the worker's child who is under the age of 16 or who is disabled before the age of 22. A disabled spouse under the age of 62 may also be able to collect benefits (unless he or she is already collecting disability benefits). The amount of benefits dependents receive is based on the worker's earnings. Dependents who work, are subject to loss of benefits of one dollar for every two dollars earned.

Survivor's Benefits. If you are a surviving spouse age 60 or over, you can collect survivor's benefits. Even if you were divorced from the decedent you can collect these benefits so long as the marriage lasted ten years. As you have probably guessed, the earlier you apply the less you earn up to age 65. As with dependent's benefits, you can also collect benefits if you are under the age of 60 so long as you are caring for the worker's child who must be under the age of 16. Surviving spouses over the age of 50 who become disabled within seven years of the worker's death can also collect from social security, as can the worker's parents who are at least age 62 and who were actually dependent on him or her for at least half of their financial support.

Divorced Spouse Retirement Benefits. If you are a "displaced homemaker", one of the many women with little or no work experience who stayed at home to raise a family and ended up divorced, you can apply for retirement benefits so long as you were married for at least ten years, have been divorced for two, and are at least 62 years old. This assumes that your ex-husband qualifies for social security. The importance of this benefit cannot be overstated. Many such displaced homemakers would receive a lower benefit based on their own earnings than they would based on their divorced spouse's earnings.

Death Benefits. If you are a surviving spouse or the surviving child of person who has died, you are probably entitled to a one time only death benefit to help defray the cost of the funeral and burial. The claim must be filed within two years of the worker's death at your local social security office.

If your claim is denied, you have the right to appeal. You may not even have to use a lawyer since you can be represented by the person of your choice. Many senior centers, as well as your local Council on Aging, have experts on social security available to help you.

The steps of an appeal are as follows:

Request For Reconsideration. Obtain the proper form for a request for reconsideration at your local social security office, fill it out and file it with the social security office. KEEP COPIES OF ALL OF YOUR PAPERWORK. Don't procrastinate; you have only 60 days from the date you received your denial within which to file your request. There is no formal hearing. All that occurs is that a different social security worker reviews your file. You can ask to speak with the reviewing staff member. He or she can agree or refuse. The decision will come to you in writing usually within 30 days. If it hasn't come within 30 days, write a letter demanding a decision.

> **NOTE**: Make all communications with the government in writing. Also, be sure to keep copies of all forms you fill out in case the original gets misplaced.

Demand A Formal Hearing. If the reconsideration doesn't go your way, request a formal hearing. Again, your local social security office will have the proper form. This hearing, called an "administrative hearing," must be demanded within 60 days of the denial that is to be reconsidered. Your demand must be in writing. The hearing is similar to a trial, you can review your entire file at the social security office, testify and present witnesses at the hearing. With so much at stake, it is probably wise to hire a lawyer if you can afford one or, at the very least, make sure your non-lawyer advocate is familiar with social security procedures.

> **NOTE**: Only hire a lawyer experienced in social security disputes. Believe it or not, you know more about social security from reading this chapter than most lawyers do. (For more on hiring and working with a lawyer, see THE LAWYER BOOK by the author, Price Stern Sloan, 1987.)

File An Appeal With The National Appeals Council. If you still haven't won, you can file an appeal with the National Appeals Council. You have 60 days to file your appeal. Your local social security office has the proper forms to fill out.

Sue. Your next step is to sue in Federal Court. You're in the big leagues now. You will definitely need a lawyer who knows what he or she is doing. Again, you have 60 days to file the lawsuit. The expenses of your fight are really going to skyrocket now, so be sure your lawyer believes your chances of success are good. Don't be afraid to get a second opinion from another lawyer.

PENSIONS

Being "with pension," is a little like being pregnant; either you are or you're not. If you are eligible for a pension, you may be entitled to either a partial payment or be "fully vested." Just as it takes time to produce a full-fledged baby, it also takes time to "earn" a pension.

The word "earn" is the right word, for that is how a pension is obtained. Pensions are an ancillary benefit of employment (meaning an addition to salary) if offered by the employer as a job benefit. There are thousands of different pension plans in effect across the United States available through private employers, unions or government services.

The Different Kinds Of Pensions: Pensions generally fall into four types: defined benefit, defined contribution, civil service and railroad retirement system.

Defined Benefit. These plans are probably the most common and are the easiest to understand. Basically you are guaranteed a specified monetary benefit when you retire. This can either be a certain amount per month for each year of service or the payment can be based on a percentage of your average salary over the years. In any event, the amount of your pension is based on a set formula, hence the term defined benefit.

Defined Contribution. Under this type of plan, the exact amount of your pension is not guaranteed ahead of time, the employer only guarantees to contribute a specified amount per employee into the pension plan. This money is then invested by the pension in order to earn money on the principal. When you retire, you are entitled to receive money based on what the employer has contributed plus a proportionate share of the earnings the plan has received over the years. Sometimes, the employer only guarantees to put in a percentage of profits rather than a specified amount. Such plans are called profit sharing plans.

At retirement, the employee can generally elect to receive monthly payments or a lump sum payment.

Civil Service Pensions. If you work for a government entity, whether it be local, state or federal, you will be earning some pretty terrific pension benefits. While each pension may vary, the amount of money you receive is based on the number of years you were employed and an average of a specified number of your highest income earning years. For example, the federal government computes the average based on the civil servant's highest three years of salary. Civil service pensions also have the following attributes which make them particularly beneficial as compared to private pensions:

—A cost of living adjustment. Most private pensions don't protect against inflation.
—Full vesting (the right to receive a full pension) after five years rather than ten or more.
—The right to "carry" your rights if you move your employment from one government entity to another.
—Early retirement, sometimes as low as 55 years.
—The right to your pension even if you are working elsewhere.

There is one drawback to a civil service pension; money collected under the system may be considered earned income by social security which can reduce your benefits.

Railroad Retirement System. This system, which is unique to railroad workers, is similar to social security since railroad workers are not covered by that plan. After ten years on the job, a railroad worker has a right to a pension at age 65, or a reduced pension at age 62. Employment for 30 years entitles the worker to retire after age 60 with no reduction in benefits. Employment for under ten years is applied to social security benefits. Some workers can collect from both social security and railroad retirement, assuming they qualify for both, although that right is currently being "squeezed" slowly toward extinction.

Features To Look For In Your Plan: If you are working toward a pension or are about to collect one, here are some of the things you need to understand in order to be sure you collect what you are entitled to:

Vesting. In order to receive pension rights under the plan, you must work for a specified period of time called the vesting period. Once you have worked the requisite number of years, you are entitled to receive a full pension when you retire. If you leave before that time, you may become what is known as partially vested, meaning you can collect a partial pension or you may simply be out of luck with no pension rights whatsoever. Thus, it is important that you understand the particulars of your own pension before you decide to quit or change jobs. Ask you plan administrator for details about how your particular plan treats vesting issues.

How The Plan Pays Benefits. Some plans give you no real choice about how you receive your benefits. Others do. These choices can be generally broken down as follows:

—Do you want a lump sum payment or monthly payments? The lump sum payment is always very tantilizing because it may consist of a lot of money, sometimes even in the hundreds of thousands of dollars. In addition, by accepting a lump sum, you are guaranteed to receive all you are entitled to since under a monthly payment schedule your death could terminate all payments. However, if you accept a lump sum payment, there may be significant income tax consequences requiring you to roll over the money into an IRA account in order to protect your nest egg.

—If you accept a monthly benefit, do you want payments to continue to your spouse after you die? Most pensions cease upon the death of the person receiving benefits. However, many plans permit beneficiaries of a pension to protect their spouses by electing to keep the pension going to the spouse for his or her life, sometimes at reduced rates should the pension receiver die. The quid pro quo for this protection is the acceptance of a lower monthly benefit. A variation on this theme is to provide a small benefit to a spouse or other beneficiary for a specified number of years after the pensioner's death.

—Does the plan offer early retirement? Somewhat akin to the early retirement option offered by social security, many pensions systems allow for their beneficiaries to retire early and receive lower benefits. Unlike social security, early retirement can be as low as age 55, with normal retirement usually being 65 years of age.

Are there any other benefits besides money? Some plans offer continuing health and life insurance coverages as well as monthly payments.

Are there any catches? Many pensions are now becoming integrated plans which does not bode well for pension holders. Integrated plans boast that they will guarantee you a certain percentage of monthly income after you retire. This level is called the goal. What they may not speak so loudly about is the fact that your social security payments are taken into consideration in guaranteeing your goal. Thus, if your goal is $1,000 a month and your social security is $545 a month then your monthly pension payment will be $455. As the years pass, your pension will probably be reduced since your social security will be going up due to cost of living increases. Under this system, if your monthly social security goes up to $585, your monthly pension payment will drop to $415, leaving you with the same $1,000 a month, which is now worth less thanks to inflation. So, as you can see, companies who provide integrated plans are not doing you a favor.

One other comment about pensions. They are controlled by federal legislation called ERISA (Employee Retirement Income Security Act). ERISA provides certain basic protections for pensioners such as insurance to protect pension funds and "rules of the game" such as limited protection of benefits for workers who have been laid off. If you are deprived of your rights, ERISA provides access to the courts for redress of grievances. For more information about your rights as the holder of a private pension contact:

U.S. Dept. of Labor
Pension and Welfare Benefits Programs
Office of Communications
Room N 4662
200 Constitution Ave. N.W
Washington D.C. 20216

NOTE: If you worked for a company that had a pension program that has gone out of business, you may still be able to collect. Contact the Pension Benefit Guaranty Coporationn, P.O. BOX 7119, Washington D.C. 20044.

INDIVIDUAL RETIREMENT ACCOUNTS

Individual Retirement Accounts, or IRAs for short, are a relatively new invention first appearing on the scene in 1981. IRAs were and are intended to promote savings and to help working men and women prepare for their retirement at the same time. They are, in essence, tax shelters for the middle class. Despite some tinkering in the Tax Reform Act of 1986 which limits the program somewhat for persons who also receive certain pensions through their place of employment, the program still performs its funtion for many wage earners quite nicely.

Here's how IRAs work: workers can deposit up to $2,000 per year ($2,250 per couple if only one is a wage earner) into an IRA account and then deduct the amount deposited from their taxable income. Interest rates that are higher than most accounts, substantial penalties for early withdrawal and the prospect of being taxed on money withdrawn serve as strong incentives to maintain the IRA until retirement. The interest earned is also tax deferred.

Over a period of ten to thirty years, quite a nice little nest egg can be saved with IRAs, frequently amounting to over six figures. Of course, the amount will vary depending upon the amount deposited and the amount of time and interest earned on the account.

At age 59 1/2, you may begin to withdraw the money from your account and you will be taxed on the principal and interest withdrawn at regular income tax rates. The point to all of this is that your tax rate then will presumably be lower than it would have been during your wage earning years. At 70 1/2 you must begin to withdraw your money according to a formula based on life expectancy. Ask the Internal Revenue Service or your accountant for further details.

NOTE: Your IRA can be invested in a bank account, mutual fund, stocks and bonds or in another way. Consult your accountant or qualified financial adviser to see which type of deposit works best for you.

If you receive a lump sum pension payment, think seriously about rolling it over (depositing it) into an IRA to avoid paying taxes on it.

INVESTING

After years of working Gladys and John Makabuck retired, sold their three bedroom house and moved into a two bedroom condominium. Their combined pensions and the profit from the sale of their house after paying for the condominium gave them $250,000—more money than they have ever had in one place in their lives. But what next? Try to parlay the loot into a cool million or play it safe? What's a couple to do?

That delightful dilemma is faced each year by tens of thousands of couples who retire and suddenly find themselves with real money for the first time in their lives. It can be a heady and sometimes dangerous feeling. Each year many of these retirees, as well as younger members of society, lose their proverbial shirts trying to play the investment game.

If you are a recent retiree and want to enter the world of investing, here are a few things experts in the field say you should know:

Remember Who You Are: Use the experience your years of living have given you. If you have worked extensively in real estate before retirement, you might take a look at that field of investment rather than deciding to take a plunge into the commodities market. If you don't know what you are doing—stay out of it!

Keep Enough "Liquidity" Available To Handle An Emergency: Liquidity is just a fancy Wall Street name for cash availability. It doesn't mean that you keep wads of dough stuffed in a mattress. It may mean, however, that you invest the "emergency fund" in a 30 to 90 day "certificate of deposit" (CD) which is money deposited in a savings institution for a specified period of time and earns a slightly higher rate of interest than a regular passbook savings account. CDs are the accounts that have a "significant interest penalty for early withdrawal." By rolling over your CDs (reinvesting into another CD upon maturity) you make money and maintain a significant liquid asset which can be quickly available in time of need.

NOTE: Make sure that your savings institution is federally insured either by the FDIC (Federal Deposit Insurance Corporation for banks) or the FSLIC (Federal Savings and Loan Corporation for savings and loans). Otherwise you could lose all of your money if the institution goes belly up as more and more are doing these days. Also, limit each account to the $100,000 maximum guaranteed by these federal agencies.

Remember "The Sleep Factor": The sleep factor asks a very important question—will you lose sleep because of the investment? If you are investing money you really can't afford to lose or the degree of risk is very high, you're better off playing it safe.

Decide What You Want From Your Investment: I can hear you snorting derisively, "What do I want? I want to make money, brightboy!" But hear me out. Some investments are principally designed to increase in value over the years while others are principally obtained to produce a steady flow of income. Some, of course, do both. Before you invest, decide what you want and make sure the investment selected is likely to obtain it for you.

Decide Whether You Want A Financial Advisor: A financial adviser's job is to analyze your financial needs such as income requirements, tax liabilities, etc. and advise you how to best manage and invest your money.

You should know that some investment advisers have a

built-in conflict of interest because they make commissions on any action you take with your investments. For example, a stockbroker makes a commission each time he or she buys or sells stock on your behalf. An unscrupulous broker may have you buy and sell stocks frequently to build up commissions. Others may charge you a straight or hourly fee, after which you still may have to pay a commission for getting into the investment. Of course, many financial advisers are worth their weight in commission statements. Just be sure you know how your financial adviser gets paid before you agree to retain him or her. If you really know what you are doing, you may wish to use a discount broker because they are merely order takers.

> **NOTE:** Financial advisers are not licensed by the state. Although there are licensed professionals such as attorneys, accountants, insurance agents, stockbrokers or the like, there is no state test or oversight of financial advisers per se. Be very careful when selecting someone who you are going to rely on to help you protect your security.
>
> You should also know something about the types of investments available. Here is a brief overview of some of the choices.

Certificates of Deposits, Money Market Accounts, etc. are accounts offered by banks and savings and loans at higher interest rates than passbook accounts.

Risk. Very low so long as the institution is federally insured and your account balance does not exceed $100,000.

Earning Potential. Will vary, depending on the economy. Ten years ago the earnings were high. As this book is written, the earnings are relatively low at between six and a half and seven and a half percent.

Government Bonds are promissory notes from government entities such as city, state or federal, that are due on a specified date and earn a specified rate of interest. They are bought and sold on the bond market.

Risk. The value of the bonds can rise and fall so there is risk involved; although, if you hold on to them long enough, they will pay their face value when due. Treasury bonds, which are bonds issued by the United States Treasury, will be extremely secure. Some municipal bonds may be less so.

Earning Potential. If the value rises after you purchase the bonds and then you sell, you make money. However, the principal attraction of government bonds, especially treasury bonds, is that they are income secure; meaning whatever their market value, the amount of interest you earn per month will not vary. Municipal bonds are tax free, but usually pay a lower interest rate.

Corporate Bonds, like government bonds, are promissory notes. However, the borrowing entity is from the private sector rather than "the people." As with government bonds, the face amount of the bond is established along with the interest rate.

Risk. The extent of risk will depend on the corporation issuing the bonds. A Standard and Poor AAA-rated corporation will be very secure (although not as secure as a treasury bond), while others who issue junk bonds (bonds issued when the company is already deep in debt, usually as part of a takeover), will be very insecure. And since they are sold on the bond market, they can go up or down in value.

Earning Potential. Usually the greater the risk, the greater the income and vise versa. The monthly payment terms will vary so be sure to read the fine print.

Ginny Maes are Government National Mortgage Association (GNMA) Bonds which are home mortgages guaranteed by the federal government.

Risk. Low since they are federally guaranteed although the price may rise or fall.

Earning Potential. Ginny Maes have a pretty good earning potential considering their safety.

> **NOTE**: Ginny Maes pay both interest and principal back to investors each month. If you invest in one be sure to set aside the principal received or you may find that you have spent your nest egg without realizing it.

Stocks are ownership interests in corporations. They are generally bought and sold in the various stock markets and often pay income based on profits to shareholders called dividends.

Risk. In a word, high. The stock market is very volatile and even an experienced player not to mention a novice, can get clobbered. If you buy on margin (where you put up part of the money and the brokerage house loans you the rest), the risk is even greater since the stock may be sold if the market goes down in order to protect the loan. This could leave you with nothing but a bad taste in your mouth.

Earning potential can be high if you buy low and sell high or sell high and buy low, which is easier said than done. Also, if you get stock in a good solid company, you can make good money on the dividends.

Mutual Funds take smaller investments and pool them together into a very large fund which is then used to invest in specific areas of the financial marketplace. The big advantage of mutual funds is professional management and its ability to diversify holdings so that losses are minimized.

Risk. These have high or low risk depending on the nature of the investments by the mutual fund and the quality of the management. The management company charges a fee that comes out of your earnings.

Earning Potential. Mutual funds can earn a fair return on your investment, depending upon the expertise of the management of the fund.

> **NOTE**:   If you are thinking of investing in a mutual fund, be sure to check out the company's track record. FORBES Magazine runs an annual issue on the subject that tracks these funds' performances.

Trust Deeds are loans to owners of real estate "secured" by the real estate itself.

Risk. It depends. TDs can be quite safe, *if* the real estate has been accurately appraised, contains sufficient equity to cover the loan in the event of sale and is fully insured for fire or other loss. However, TDs can be very risky especially if you have a second or third TD, which means that you collect behind the first creditors in the event of default. Also, in the past there has been a lot of fraud such as false appraisals that left the TD holder secured by nothing. If you are not familiar with real estate transactions, it is a good idea not to invest in TDs.

Earning potential. TDs can earn a good piece of cash depending on the interest rate charged.

There are other types of investments such as options and commodities that can either be extremely risky or relatively safe. Just be sure to keep a strong eye on SAFETY if you do invest, since you may not be able to earn lost money again. Do not invest in an unfamiliar area. Remember that when it comes to investments, caveat emptor, which means BUYER BEWARE.

> **NOTE**: The discussion about investments has been intended as a broad overview of the subject only. It is not complete nor does it list every risk that can be expected. It is also not intended as an investment guide.

EMPLOYMENT

When it comes to putting bread on the table, many seniors still have to do it the old fashioned way; they must "eeaaarnnn it." The trouble is that where work was once plentiful, it may now be scarce. In younger years, opportunities for employment may have been bountiful; now they may be more limited. Where employment was once pursued as a career, it must now be thought of as a job.

An unpleasant fact of senior life is the difficulty in finding interesting and gainful employment after retirement. The sad truth is that many employers simply don't take senior citizens seriously in terms of their wish to work, their need to work or the contributions they can make to the employment environment. So many of the jobs offered to seniors are menial, sporadic or so low-paying they may not be worth the effort.

However, while all this may be true generically as applied to a broad statistical group, it's not necessarily true for you as an individual. If you want to work, realize that you are an individual and not a statistic. You can find a good and enjoyable job. Here are some tips that I hope will ease the process:

Take Inventory Of Yourself: Honestly assess your physical, mental and emotional conditions and what you are looking for in a job. Get a good handle on what it is you can and cannot do and what you want and don't want to do. Ask yourself the following questions to prepare yourself for your search:

—"How much money do I need to make?" Your financial situation will probably define how picky you can be about the job you take. Obviously, if you are in dire straights you are more willing to take a job that does not send shivers of joy down your spine than you would be if financial considerations are secondary to the social and emotional rewards of employment.

—"What job would I love?" and "What job will I be willing to take?" The answers to these two questions will define the parameters of your search.

—"How far from home am I willing to work?" The answer to this question will depend on matters such as your health and physical abilities, your responsibilities at home and on the availability of transportation. If you are limited to a five-mile radius from home, the best job in the world that is twenty miles away just isn't the job for you.

—"What days and hours are you willing to work?" A job that requires you to work weekends when you are not willing to do so is clearly not worth applying for. If you are willing to work unusual hours, your search may prove to be easier.

—"What is my experience?" The answer to this question involves far more than a job title or description; it's the essence of what you actually have done. For example, suppose you were a supervisor in your past employment. Telling a prospective employer that fact does not tell the whole story. Who did you supervise? A small office or a large factory? Did you train people, fire them or judge their work? You must be prepared to tell the prospective employer the truth beneath the job description in a way that will communicate in a professional way, "You need me, Buster!"

—"What are my skills?" Perhaps your strong suit is organization. If so, be prepared to tell the interviewer and have examples ready to illustrate your claim. Maybe you are a "people" person who is just right for that front office position. Be ready to prove it.

—"Why do I want to work?" Many employers may not understand why you want to work. There's nothing wrong with saying you need the money. You can also say you enjoy the feeling of being productive and contributing toward a positive endeavor. Whatever your reasons, the answer to this question says a lot about whether you are the kind of person who will fit into the job environment.

Realize That You May Need Help: Many seniors are unprepared for the trauma of job hunting. Although they may have had long-term careers where they measured their work for an employer in decades rather than years, they have not had the experience of looking for work in a very long time. In addition, the jobs that are available are not always easy to find. Many seniors may also need to learn how to communicate the usefulness of their past job experience to a prospective employer in a different field. These skills are taught to seniors in programs such as "Job Club" and "Operation Able." Don't hesitate to join a job support group. After all, the enthusiasm of others can go a long way in giving you the pep to give it your all. To find an employment program or support group in your area contact your local Agency on Aging, the local chapter of the AARP or a local community college.

Be Willing To Take No For An Answer: That doesn't mean to be passive. On the contrary, it means just the opposite. Think of yourself as a salesperson. As any salesperson will tell you, no's are just part of the job. You simply have to plow through ten "nos" before you get a "yes." If you are serious in your desire, you won't give up until you reach your goal.

Learn To Read The Signs: There is a difference between being aggressive and wasting your time, but sometimes, the dividing line may be hard to pin down. For instance, Job Club, a nation-wide employment assistance training service, teaches its students to watch out for the following "Buy Signs" (go for it) and "Bye Signs" (move on to greener pastures) when you are applying for a job.

BUY SIGNS
"What experience do you have?" This question indicates interest and an open mind.

BYE SIGNS
"Send a resume." Meaning, I don't have the guts to say I'm not interested. (Send your resume anyway; they might mean it.)

BUY SIGNS (continued)	**BYE SIGNS**
"Where have you worked?" Things are getting warmer.	"Come in and apply." See above.
"Tell me about your last job." . . . warmer.	"You're not qualified." It's going to be hard to change a mind.
"What can you do for me?" Be ready to hit a home run and score!	"We already have someone in mind." In other words, we don't want you.

Don't Be Afraid To Blow Your Own Horn: Your employer wants you to be the right person for them. However, they must be convinced that you are "the one". The only person who can persuade them is you. It is not bragging to promote your own abilities, but it is self-defeating not to.

Don't Take Rejection Personally: Remember, no's are part of the process. Do not take it personally if a prospective employer decides to pass. If you allow a "no" to lower your self-esteem, you will be communicating this negativity to the interviewer and will be creating a downward spiral of self-fulfilling prophesy.

Dig For The Jobs: Contrary to popular belief, the classified section is not necessarily the first place to look for work. In fact, the classifieds are often the last place employers turn when looking to fill a slot. Don't be afraid to call companies or walk in to apply for a job. Set yourself a goal of at least two interviews a week and go out and make it happen. Send thank you notes even if rejected and follow up at locales where you sensed some interest.

The good news is that increasingly, there is help available. Both private and public resources are being devoted to making the task of finding work easier. Here are just a few examples of what is being done:

The Un-retired Program: Travelers Insurance Company has created the Un-retirement Program specifically to provide senior citizens with temporary employment opportunities. In addition to providing placement, the program will also provide some training. If you are interested, contact:

> The Travelers Companies
> Un-Retirement Plan
> Personnel-Administrative Dept.
> One Tower Square
> Hartford, CT. 06101

In addition, corporations such as McDonalds and Thrifty Drugs are actively seeking senior job applicants

"The Senior Aides Program": The National Council Of Senior Citizens operates this program under the Senior Community Service Employment Program of the U.S. Dept. Of Labor under The Older Americans Act. The program is designed to assist low income seniors find employment in community service jobs including home health care, teacher assistance, paralegal and consumer affairs, to name a few. Currently some 10,000 older Americans are provided employment under the program. For information, contact your state or local Department of Aging or:

> National Council Of Senior Citizens
> 925 15th St. N.W.
> Washington D.C. 20005
> (202) 347-8800

Local Dept. Of Aging Programs: Most big cities have an employment service especially for older workers. These nonprofit agencies work to develop jobs for seniors as well as help them in jobs. In Los Angeles, the program is run by the Los Angeles Council on Careers for Older Americans. In Philadelphia, there is the Senior Employment and Educational Service. But whatever the title, there will often be a place to turn to for help in finding work. These organizations can also refer you to support groups such as Jobs Clubs.

> **NOTE:** Whether you are still working in your career or looking for a job after a period of retirement, it is illegal under federal law to discriminate against you because of your age unless there is an occupational qualification exception. It is now illegal to force someone to retire or to deny them benefits such as health insurance due to age. It is also illegal to discriminate with regard to wages, layoffs and promotions. In addition, many state laws also prohibit age discrimination.
>
> Of course, the truth is that discrimination happens all of the time. If you feel it has happened to you, contact your State Department of Aging or the Federal EEOC (Equal Employment Opportunity Commission) for details on the law and grievance procedures.

HOME EQUITY CONVERSION

Home Equity Conversion, which was briefly discussed in Chapter One, isn't really income, it's a loan. However, you would never know it because instead of paying monthly payments, you receive them.

In essence, a Home Equity Conversion is a loan on the equity in your home (the difference between what you owe on the property and what it is worth). Rather than receive the money all at once and then have to make payments, you receive the loan proceeds in monthly increments depending on the value of the property and the terms of the conversion agreement.

The most common form of conversion is a reverse mortgage that allows you to receive monthly payments while retaining ownership and possession of your home. For some, this cash can mean the difference between a relatively carefree retirement and one that is fraught with worry. Reverse mortgages usually have the following common characteristics:

—The total amount you owe grows larger with each payment you receive. Thus, instead of your debt shrinking each month, it grows based on the principal you receive and interest charged upon it. Over the years, this debt can become substantial.

—As stated above, the amount you receive depends on the equity of your home and the length of the loan term.

—You can usually have the first payment fairly large so that you can pay off pre-existing loans or repair the property.

—All reverse mortgages become due and payable by your estate when you die, when you permanently move out of your home or when you sell. Most will also have some provision protecting you in the event of an extended stay in a nursing home.

—If you have problems repaying the loan, the only asset that can be attached is your home itself.

The disadvantages of reverse mortgages include the loss of equity for your heirs, the increased cost of the loan over conventional mortgages and the fact that money received from a reverse mortgage can affect your eligibility for Medicaid and Supplemental Security Income if not spent during the month it is received.

Somewhat akin to the reverse mortgage are the Sale Leaseback and the Life Estate types of equity conversions. Both involve sale of your property instead of loans, but also put cash in your pocket on a monthly basis.

In the sale leaseback arrangement, you sell your house to a person or entity who becomes your landlord. You have the right to live in the house for the rest of your life (usually accomplished by having a lease term in excess of your life expectancy). Your rent is usually less than the monthly payments you receive as part of the sale and thus you come out with cash in your pocket each month. In this regard, make sure the lease protects you from unreasonable rent increases that could eat up your monthly income. Repairs, property taxes and insurance are now your new landlord's responsibility.

In a life estate, you remain the owner of your home until you die. What you sell is the "remainder interest" or right to ownership upon your death. These plans are usually financed by nonprofit organizations and/or government entities. Under life estate conversions, you are responsible for taxes, repairs and all incidentals of ownership. On the other hand, you are not dependent on a landlord to fulfill these legal duties. The amount you receive for your remainder interest varies but is usually less than a reverse mortgage.

NOTE: Home equity conversions are complicated contracts involving the ownership of your home and potential tax consequences. In addition, the value of the contract to you will be directly based upon the language of the contract you enter into. You should hire a lawyer who is experienced with home equity conversions when negotiating your deal. For more detailed information, contact the AARP or:

National Center For Home Equity
Conversion
110 East Main St.
Madison, Wis. 53703
(608) 256-2111

SUPPLEMENTAL SECURITY INCOME

Supplemental Security Income (SSI) is a joint federal/state income assistance program that is administered by the Social Security Administration. You need not qualify for social security to be eligible to receive SSI. The program is available to low income seniors and to the blind or disabled of any age.

In order to qualify for SSI assistance you have to be very poor. You can only own assets of $1,500 or $2,250 for a couple (excluding your home and car). The income threshold permitted to qualify for benefits is low and varies from state to state. (Social security is regarded as income).

As you would expect, if you receive SSI and find employment, your benefits will be reduced—one dollar for every two dollars you earn. Your benefits can also be reduced if you receive support such as food or shelter from another source.

To apply for SSI, go to your nearest social security office.

> **NOTE**: If you qualify for SSI, you may also qualify for other government assistance such as food stamps and housing subsidies. Contact your nearest department of aging or social welfare office for details.

3

If You've Got Your Health, You've Got Everything

Medical Care And The Senior Citizen

The Importance Of The Primary Care Physician;
Preventative Care; Accident Prevention; Senior
Public Health Enemies; Hospitals and Seniors;
Home Health Care

According to the Bible, mankind is given threescore and ten years (70 years) within which to engage in that mysterious dance called life. Modern scientists are a little more optimistic, estimating that if we play our cards right, our natural life span should average approximately 85 years. Indeed, since the turn of the century, the average life span in the United States has risen from 47 to 73 years.

Many believe that the most we can hope to accomplish regarding Old Man Death is to delay his inevitable appearance. But there's more we can do to extend the length of our stay here. A major factor in creating a long and satisfying life in the senior years is quality health care. In a sense, your body is a lot like your car; change the oil regularly, get a tuneup when needed, avoid accidents and hopefully you'll get hundreds of thousands of miles of happy motoring—or living, as the case may be. In other words, you take good care of your body and chances are your body will take good care of you.

THE IMPORTANCE OF YOUR PRIMARY CARE PHYSICIAN

Regardless of age, each and every one of us should have a doctor to call our own. This doctor, called the primary care physician, is in essence the gatekeeper of your health. Besides being available for you, his or her duties are:

To Establish A Plan Of Preventative Care: Ben Franklin, one of the world's most famous and productive senior citizens once said, "A stitch in time saves nine." Well, he could have been describing your doctor's attitude about your health. The whole idea behind preventative care is to catch and mend any "rip" that may appear in the fabric of your health before it causes the loss of a seam. This is done through regular physicals and screening tests.

The Maintenance Of "Chronic Conditions": Until very recently "acute" illnesses such as influenza (548,000 people died in the epidemic of 1918 alone), polio, diptheria and tuberculosis were the primary causes of death. As we approach the 21st century, our principal enemy is now the chronic disease that works slowly and steadily over a period of time, such as hypertension, arthritis and diabetes. Your doctor's primary function is to keep these monsters under as much control as possible so that they do the least harm.

Patient Education: When it comes to your health, what you don't know can and does hurt you. Your doctor is there to educate you about staying healthy and counsel you when you become ill.

Referrals To Other Doctors: Sometimes your doctor may need to call in a reinforcement called a sub-specialist for problems that go beyond his area of expertise. For example, if you have a heart problem, he or she may send you to see a cardiologist who deals excusively with heart problems. Your personal physician should not only tell you when you should see a sub-specialist but should be able to refer you to the best since most doctors know the quality physicians in the community as well as the ones to avoid. In addition, if you are being treated by a sub-specialist, your doctor should follow up to make sure things are going smoothly.

Hand-Holding: Often if you're a grandparent, you may need someone who can soothe your fears and tell you everything is going to be alright. A big part of your doctor's job is simply to be there if you have a question or need a helping hand.

Advocacy: As you will see in Chapter Four, health care is becoming a jungle for many seniors. Insurance companies, Medicare and hospitals sometimes make it tougher rather than easier to get quality health care based on your needs as an individual. In such cases, you should be able to rely on your doctor to come to the rescue and assert your case for prolonged hospitalization or increased medical care.

For your personal physician, you should have either an internist or a family practice specialist. An internist is a physician who diagnoses and "medically" (i.e. non-surgically) treats diseases of adults. A family practitioner is a doctor who specializes in general family care and has training in pediatrics, general surgery, psychiatry, obstetrics as well as internal medicine. The difference between the two can best be described as the difference between "depth" (internal medicine) and "breadth" (family practice). The type of doctor you select is up to you.

Whichever type of doctor you choose, be sure that the physician has a deep interest in geriatrics (the treatment of older people). This is important because your medical needs change as you get older. Here are a few things to ask your doctor:

—Are you board certified? When looking for a personal physician, be sure to ask if the physician is board certified. This means that the doctor has passed medical school, completed internship, fulfilled at least four years of residency and passed a national test called "the boards." A doctor who is not board certified should at least be "board qualified," which means he or she is eligible to take the test and has not yet taken it or else has failed. While a doctor who has failed may be a fine physician, the fact of the failure is something you have the right to know.

—Do you go to nursing homes? At some point in many seniors' lives a stay at a nursing home may become a necessity. Most stays are not permanent, but whether yours is or not, you definitely want to be able to keep your personal physician. If your doctor "doesn't do nursing homes," than he or she is simply not willing to give you 100% of your potential necessary care. The time to find that little fact out is before, not after you develop a strong trusting relationship.

—Do you like taking care of senior citizens? Some doctors have a deep love for treating older people, others do not. Obviously you should find a doctor who enjoys serving you. In addition, the medical care given older patients frequently differs from that given to someone who is younger, even though the disease or malady may be the same. It is a major benefit for you to have a doctor whose practice emphasizes senior care.

—Do you take continuing education courses in geriatrics? Medicine is in a constant state of growth with information expanding at a breathtaking pace. If your doctor is not keeping up with the changes in geriatric case management, he or she may quickly fall behind the times and you will be the one to suffer.

NOTE: There is a new certification offered for internists and family care practitioners who emphasize geriatrics in their practice. If your doctor has this special certification in geriatrics it means that he or she has enough experience and knowledge to pass a rigorous test specifically geared to the medical needs of senior citizens.

PREVENTATIVE CARE

The best thing you can do to optimize your health care is to keep from getting sick in the first place or, at the very least, catch problems while they are still treatable. This defensive medicine is called "preventative care."

EDUCATE YOURSELF:

The first step of preventative care is educating yourself about your body and its needs. Many senior organizations have educational booklets that cover everything from nutrition to exercise to the warning signs that things may be going wrong. For example, the AARP has a booklet called "Pep Up Your Life," that has excellent tips on strengthening your muscles and increasing flexibility. Your doctor will also be able to give you materials to help you out. Senior centers offer many educational opportunities in health care. The American Cancer Society, the American Heart Association and consumer groups like Public Citizen Health Research Group or The Peoples Medical Society also offer invaluable advice and informational services.

CHECKUPS AND SCREENING TESTS:

Besides educating yourself about your body and health, you and your doctor should also establish a course of preventative checkups and screenings. These should be specifically designed to suit your needs based on your health, medical and family history and any other criteria agreed upon between you and your doctor. The preventative tests and procedures listed below are based upon guidelines recommended by the American Heart Association and the American Cancer Society and other experts in the field. They are intended as rules of thumb only and may not apply to your individual case. As stated above, your individual needs for preventative care may differ. In addition, your doctor may recommend tests not listed here.

Immunizations: Decide with your doctor whether or not you need yearly flu shots or any other innoculation.

History: Your health history, which is often as important to a successful diagnosis as the symptoms, should be taken every two and one-half years after age 61 and annually after age 75 for healthy individuals.

Mammogram: A mammogram is a photograph of the breast made by an X-ray which searches for indications of cancer too small to locate manually. This test is recommended once between the ages of 35 and 40 to get a baseline and then every two years until age 50. Thereafter, an annual test is recommended. Self-examination for lumps is recommended on a monthly basis.

Stool Slide Tests: This is an analysis of the stool to search for hidden traces of blood, the appearance of which could mean cancer or some other disorder in the digestive tract. Stool slide tests are recommended once a year for everyone over 50.

Sigmoidoscopies: A sigmoidoscopy allows a physician to see within the colon by means of a flexible tube. While the test is uncomfortable, it can prove invaluable at catching cancer at a very early stage when it is far more treatable. (I know from first-hand experience how important this procedure is. The failure of my father to obtain a sigmoidoscopy may have led to a late diagnosis of the colon cancer that took his life.) The American Cancer Society recommends that both men and women receive this test once every three years after two normal exams one year apart starting at age 50.

Urinalysis: The urine is a veritable road map of the workings of many vital organs. It is recommended that a urinalysis be performed every year after the age of 40.

Blood Tests: Like urine, the blood is a window to the workings of the body. Blood tests should be taken every five years until age 60 and every two-and-a-half years thereafter if good baselines have been documented.

Blood Pressure: Readings should be obtained by a healthy person who shows no symptoms of high blood pressure or heart disease every two-and-a-half to five years until age 61, and then every two-and-a-half years until age 75 whereupon it should be taken annually.

Pelvic Examinations: All healthy women over the age of 40 should have a pelvic exam once a year.

EKGs: The American Heart Association recommends a baseline EKG at ages 20, 40 and 60.

Physical Exams: The rate of physicals varies depending on what your physician is looking for. The newest American Heart Association guidelines have moved away from recommending an annual physical to a thorough heart and vascular system checkup every five years until age 50, every two-and-one-half years until age 75 and annually thereafter.

The American Cancer Society recommends an examination for cancers of the thyroid, testicles, prostate, ovaries, lymph nodes and skin every three years until age 40. Thereafter it is recommended that you be screened yearly for cancer.

> **NOTE:** These are only general guidelines which may not apply to you. Moreover, they do not constitute all of the tests and exams which may be available. Be sure to ask your doctor to establish a specific preventative care guideline designed for you.

All these suggestions may sound great, but suppose you don't have the money to pay for them? Since Medicare and many traditional health insurance policies do not pay for preventative care, this can be a problem. However, I encourage you to work with your doctor to get as much screening assistance as possible. Perhaps your doctor can find a "diagnosis" which would require a screening. Medicare may then pay or else you could work out a schedule of payments to your doctor. In any case, do not stint on your well-being because once health is lost it may be difficult to find again.

ACCIDENT PREVENTION:

In the old silent films, people could run into trains, wreck cars or fall down a flight of stairs and bounce right back to get a pie in the face in the last reel. Real life, however, is quite different, especially for the elderly. People aged 65 and older constitute 11% of the population, yet according to Dr. Garrett Snipes, a clinical instructor in family medicine and geriatrics at Florida Hospital, Orlando, they suffer 25% of all fatal accidents. Moreover, he adds, when an elderly person is hospitalized because of an accident, the stay is usually longer and recovery slower than in a younger person.

That being the case, it behooves all senior citizens to do all within their power to keep from becoming an accident statistic.

Here are some tips that can help pave the way to a safe and sane senior experience.

—Make sure that flooring and carpeting are in good condition and firmly secured to the floor. Loose rugs and "snags" are falls waiting to happen. Kitchen floors should be make of non-slip materials.

—Stairs should be well lit with the top and bottom steps painted. Each step should have a nonskid tread. Make sure the bannister is strong.

—Night-lights should be placed in areas such as bathrooms or kitchens where an older person is likely to walk at night. At other times each room should be well lit.

—Telephones should be conveniently positioned so that no one has to rush or stumble over furniture to answer the phone.

—Railings should be installed in bathtubs and if necessary, by the toilet.

—Use a good bathmat or have a nonslip surface installed in the tub or on the floor. Have a seat in the tub.

—Hot and cold faucets in the bathroom should be very clearly marked.

—Do not use low couches or furniture on casters.

—Try to control the activity of pets to avoid tripping.

—Have stove controls clearly marked.

—Have smoke alarms installed throughout the home.

—Wear proper shoes with low heels that are well fitting.

—Do not use extension cords that can be tripped over.

—Use a sturdy step stool when reaching in high places.

—Receive proper training in the use of a cane or walker. Improper use leads to falls.

Be especially careful if you or a loved one has been suffering dizzy spells, weakness, fainting or any balance difficulties. If there are problems with vision or coordination, falls are a particular hazard. If you are on medication, make sure you know whether it can cause problems such as drowsiness or depression (as do many blood pressure medications).

SENIOR MALADIES

While each stage of life has its joys, it also brings its afflictions. So it is not surprising that certain physical difficulties are more common in older people than they are in younger ones. Smart seniors recognize these common enemies and are ever vigilant in the defense of their own good health.

SENIOR PUBLIC ENEMY #1—ALZHEIMER'S DISEASE:
Alzheimer's Disease is an insidious form of dementia caused by a deterioration of brain cells. It strikes older people with such frequency that it is one of the leading causes of death in the United States. Approximately two and a half million Americans suffer from the condition.

Symptoms: Alzheimer's usually begins gradually with problems remembering recent events or difficulty performing familiar tasks. As the disease progresses, the victim may undergo a severe change in personality and have difficulty following directions or remembering family members. Ultimately, the sufferer becomes unable to care for him or herself.

> **NOTE:** Not all memory problems or similar difficulties are symptomatic of Alzheimer's.

Prognosis: Unfortunately, not good. Alzheimer's is a fatal disease with no known cure and no treatment currently available to stop the slow progress of the affliction. If you or a loved one has been diagnosed by a competent physician and have obtained a second opinion that the problems are probably a result of Alzheimer's (there is no 100% diagnosis except during an autopsy), you should:

Get a Second Opinion: Consider consulting with a neurologist and/or a geriatric psychologist to triple check the diagnosis. Severe depression has, on occassion, been misdiagnosed as Alzheimer's.

Join The Alzheimer's Disease and Related Disorders Association (ADRDA): This wonderful organization assists victims and the families of victims with support groups, educational seminars, pamphlets, books and advise on the care and nurturing of the victim and the caregiver alike. There is a chapter of ADRDA in most cities. You can contact the Alzheimer's Hotline at (800) 621-0379 or in Illinois at (800) 572-6037.

Adjust Your Life: Once a victim knows the score, he or she can make adjustments so as to maximize his or her potential. For example, ADRDA recommends that victims start to write things down to supplement lost memory. Another ADRDA tip is to make a habit of leaving important items such as glasses, dentures, purse and the like in one easy to find place. Also, victims and families should take note of where that place is. Above all, victims and families must be patient with themselves and be willing to accept help.

Plan Ahead: Since the disease progresses slowly, sufferers who have been diagnosed as probable victims sometimes have time to make plans concerning their care and estate. Areas to deal with include retirement, legal affairs, support services, living arrangements and what, if any, extraordinary measures should be taken to keep the victim alive. Such planning is certainly not fun, but it is definitely necessary.

> **NOTE:** Many ADRDA chapters are beginning to offer an I.D. bracelet for victims of the disease at a nominal cost. The bracelet identifies the wearer and gives a phone number to call where vital information about the victim can be found.

SENIOR PUBLIC ENEMY #2 - ARTHRITIS:

Arthritis is a major crippler of older people. Depending on its severity, arthritis can turn everyday activities such as simply getting out of bed into excruciatingly painful ones. Today, over 31 million Americans suffer from some form of arthritis. There is no cure.

Symptoms: By far the most common type of arthritis is degenerative arthritis. Sufferers of this disease experience pain in the joints of the hands, knees, hips or feet. They may also suffer muscle and back pain. Sufferers of a "systemic" type of arthritis such as rheumatoid arthritis may also suffer things such as weight loss and fever.

Prognosis: Your primary care physician can treat the pain in most cases. In others, sufferers of the disease may need to see a specialist like a rheumatologist or an orthopedist. Doctors can prescribe pain medication, beginning with simple aspirin, and can also give medication to reduce swelling. Proper exercise or prescribed physical therapy can also help. In a few cases, a badly damaged joint can be surgically replaced, most notably the hip. The Arthritis Foundation can also be of assistance by offering informational and educational services as well as putting victims in touch with support groups and discount pharmacy services. They can also help find exercise programs, such as "Twinges in the Hinges" to help strengthen the body. There is a local chapter of the Arthritis Foundation near you.

PUBLIC SENIOR ENEMY #3 -
HEART DISEASE AND HEART ATTACK:

There are far too many types of heart disease to include in a general discussion such as this. However, the most common type is really a disease of arteries called arteriolsclorisis, better known as hardening of the arteries. This condition is caused by plaque building up in the coronary arteries which slowly cuts off the blood supply to the heart muscle and can lead to a heart attack. Heart disease is the leading cause of death in older Americans.

Symptoms: Any pain or feeling of fullness or squeezing in the chest that lasts more than two minutes should be considered as a possible heart attack. Also, pain in the shoulder or jaw can be the sign of a heart attack. Vomiting and sweating frequently accompany the pain. Older people may also suffer silent symptoms rather than painful ones. In such cases, the person may simply feel breathless or suffer a sudden state of confusion or change in mental status without chest pain. Heart disease may be symptomless and only reveal itself under EKG or cholesterol blood count.

Prognosis: There is a lot you can do to prevent heart disease. Often a simple change in diet to reduce cholesterol is the first step. Your doctor may also want you to engage in a regular exercise program such as walking or riding a stationary bike. Your doctor and The American Heart Association will be able to educate you fully on heart disease and about things you can do to avoid or reduce its effects.

PUBLIC SENIOR ENEMY #4 - HYPERTENSION

Hypertension, also known as high blood pressure, occurs when the blood flows through the system at such high pressure that it causes damage to blood vessels and vital organs such as the kidneys. Hypertension is a major cause of stroke (the bleeding or clotting of a blood vessel of the brain which damages the brain due to loss of oxygen or other nutrients). Strokes present themselves with a sudden weakness or numbness of the face, arm, leg or one side of the body. These indicators may or may not be temporary. There may also be a slurring of words, loss of speech or unexplained dizziness or falls. (A friend of mine had a stroke; his symptom was a loss in his ability to read). Hypertension can also lead to kidney failure and the loss of use of other organs.

Symptoms: Hypertension is called, "the silent killer" because it usually has no symptoms. That's why it's so very important to have your blood pressure checked on a regular basis.

Prognosis: Hypertension is usually controllable with a reduction of salt in the diet, change of diet, loss of weight, regular exercise and, if necessary, medication. When medications are necessary, be sure you work closely with your doctor and report all side effects. Finding the right drug and dosage is done by a ruling out process. Your doctor and The American Heart Association can give you detailed information about hypertension and the other illnesses caused by this condition.

> **NOTE:** The medications which control hypertension are always being improved to produce lower side effects. Your job as a patient is to make sure you have a doctor who keeps up-to-date on these changes.

SENIOR PUBLIC HEALTH ENEMY #5-DIABETES:
Diabetes is a disease of the pancreas which prevents it from producing enough insulin to convert food into energy. As a result, glucose (blood sugar) cannot enter cells, so it builds

up in the blood. Diabetes can lead to blindness, a loss of limbs and death. There are two types of diabetes, "insulin dependent" which used to be called "juvenile onset" and "non-insulin dependent" which attacks many seniors.

Symptoms: The most common early syptoms are increased thirst and frequent urination. Other symptoms include increased appetite, infections of the skin or urinary tract, slow healing of cuts and bruises, lack of energy, pain or numbness in the legs or feet and blurred vision. Symptoms of non-insulin dependent or "mature onset" diabetes may have little or no symptoms at all.

Prognosis: Some victims only have to watch their diets by eating less sugar and fat and eating more carbohydrates and fiber. Others must take insulin injections. In some cases, oral medications are all that are needed. All victims must monitor their conditions closely. For more details contact your local chapter of the American Diabetes Association or consult your doctor.

PUBLIC ENEMY #6 - CANCER:

Cancer is an insidious disease that comes in many sizes, shapes and forms. It can present itself as a tumor, as with colon and breast cancer; as a skin lesion or as a condition of the blood such as leukemia. It is a killer but can be cured in many cases with early detection.

Symptoms: There are too many types of cases to list all of the symptoms here. However, you should familiarize yourself with the following "The Seven Danger Signals of Cancer" as developed by The American Cancer Society:

1) change in bowel or bladder habits
2) a sore that does not heal
3) unusual bleeding or discharge
4) thickening or lump in breast or elsewhere

5) indigestion or difficulty in swallowing
6) obvious change in wart or mole
7) nagging cough or hoarseness.

(Reprinted with the permission of The American Cancer Society.)

Prognosis: Cancer treatments range from chemotherapy to radiation to surgery or a combination of two or all three. Many believe that the patient's attitude is also important. The best selling book *Love, Medicine, and Miracles* by Dr. Bernie Siegel discusses this in detail. Regardless of treatment, early detection is definitely the key to a successful outcome so be sure to see a doctor if you have any doubts whatsoever. Also, be sure you obtain good ongoing preventative care.

> **NOTE:** If you have questions about cancer, call the American Cancer Society hotline toll free at (800) 4 - CANCER.

SENIOR PUBLIC HEALTH ENEMY #7- HEARING LOSS:

Up to 50% of seniors up to age 79 suffer from some form of hearing loss. This can be temporary or permanent or caused as a side effect of some medications. Many people allow vanity to keep them from reporting hearing loss to their doctors which is unfortunate since many types of hearing difficulties are easily treated.

Symptoms: Hearing loss has fairly obvious symptoms: words become difficult to understand, normal conversational tones sound muffled, the sufferer begins speaking too loudly and frequently has to ask others to repeat themselves. Hearing loss may also make an older person appear to be confused, unintelligent or uncooperative which can lead to depression and withdrawal.

Prognosis: Hearing aids can provide relief for many at a

reasonably low cost. Often surgery can correct the problem and sometimes all that is needed is a flushing out of ear wax.

> **NOTE:** The Johns Hopkins Hospital Hearing and Speech Clinic offers a free hearing screening test over the phone (toll not included). Call (301) 955-3434 twenty-four hours a day for the test. If you fail any part of it, call your doctor.

SENIOR PUBLIC HEALTH ENEMY #8 -
REDUCTION OR LOSS OF SIGHT:

Many seniors experience increased difficulty with vision as they grow older. This can be a simple problem such as nearsightedness that can be corrected with reading glasses to more severe problems, that can lead to blindness like glaucoma and cataracts.

Symptoms: Anything that reduces vision such as inability to read, a "clouding" or haziness in the vision or "rainbow rings" around lights can indicate vision impairment. There may be no symptoms, especially with glaucoma, so regular eye checkups are a definite must.

Prognosis: Sometimes all that is required is a new pair of glasses or eye drops. For more serious problems, surgery may be recommended. Early detection is vital in the treatment of serious eye disorders.

> **NOTE:** Even if you can't afford eye care, you can receive help at no cost (whether or not you qualify for medicare) through the "National Eye Care Project" sponsored by the American Academy of Ophthalmology and its participating physicians. Contact your local area agency or senior center to get the names of participating doctors in your area.

> Cataract surgery is sometimes per-
> formed unnecessarily when lesser treat-
> ment would suffice. Even though such sur-
> gery is done on a routine basis throughout
> the country, treat the procedure as serious-
> ly as you would any other surgery. Make
> sure your ophthamologist is reputable and
> always get a second opinion.

SENIOR PUBLIC HEALTH ENEMY #9 - INCONTINENCE:

Incontinence is the involuntary loss of control over urine, stool or both. The loss can be minor, such as leakage of a small amount of urine upon sneezing (stress incontinence) to a total inability to control elimination functions. There are four causes of the condition: urological, (medical problems in the genito-urinary tract), neurological (disease of the brain, spine or nerves), psychological (depression, anxiety, etc.) and environmental factors such as a handicap that prevent access to a bathroom or as a side effect of certain medications.

Symptoms: Full or partial inability to control bladder or bowel functions indicates incontinence.

Prognosis: Treatment for incontinence can range from surgery to medications to devices such as catheters. There are also special undergarments that allow the sufferer to lead a normal life. HIP (Help For Incontinent People) is a national organization that services the needs of incontinent patients and provides easy access to information about the products available for sufferers. HIP can be reached at P.O. Box 544, Union, South Carolina, 29379 or at (803)585-8789.

SENIOR PUBLIC HEALTH ENEMY #10 - THE "IT'S ONLY OLD AGE SYNDROME:"

This form of negligence arises from a belief by many doctors and other health care professionals that your health problems are a result of old age.

Symptoms: The most obvious symptom is refusal to take your health complaints seriously.

Prognosis: First of all, you should find a doctor who understands and respects the health needs of older people. Insist on being treated with respect and courtesy. Obtain second opinions if necessary, and always be vigilant against this particular form of discrimination because it creates needless suffering to thousands, perhaps millions of people.

There are other common senior problems such as impotence, prostate conditions (which affect most older men to a greater or lesser degree), osteoporosis and depression. The key to dealing with any problem that may arise is 1) finding a good doctor who cares about you; 2) obtaining the information you need to make informed decisions about treatment, and especially; 3) an attitude that says, "This will not get me down." Dr. James Davis, Assistant Professor, Division of Geriatric Medicine told me, "The most vigorous and happiest older people I see are those that keep themselves mentally and emotionally involved with life regardless of their physical condition. I've seen blind people who can't even get out of bed lead very happy and fulfilling lives." Or to quote that great philosopher and All Star Catcher, Yogi Berra, "It ain't over 'til it's over."

HOSPITALS

Sooner or later you or a loved one may have to spend some time in a hospital. When this occurs, you don't want to enter just any hospital. There are hospitals that make special efforts to serve the needs of seniors, and then there are just hospitals. Assuming you have a choice, you want to enter the right hospital to maximize your health care. Here are some things to look for in a hospital.

MEDICAL EXCELLENCE:

How do you find a hospital that provides medical excellence? After all, you can't just call and ask, "Is your hospital any good?" That would be like calling a restaurant and asking if they mean it when their sign says, "Fine Food." You can learn a lot about any hospital before you agree to enter if you ask some of the following questions:

—Ask your doctor why he or she is sending you to a particular hospital. Whether you are being treated by your primary care physician or some other doctor, it is his or her responsibility to recommend a hospital suitable to your needs. Your choice is usually limited to one in which your doctor is permitted to practice, which is called being ("on staff"). Your doctor will probably be on staff at several local hospitals. Your job, or that of someone who is assisting you, is to make sure that your doctor's recommendation is based on solid reasons such as the quality of the nursing staff or the excellence of the critical care unit that will benefit your health care and not just for the convenience of the doctor or because he or she may "own a piece of the action." In addition to the question listed above, you should also find out about whether the hospital has a problem with hospital-acquired infection (where you come out of the hospital with an infection or medical problem you didn't have when you went in) whether their nurses are well trained and whether the hospital is well equipped to handle any complications you may experience.

—Ask the hospital administration what their JCAH Accreditation is. JCAH stands for Joint Commission on Accreditation of Hospitals. One of their functions is to inspect hospitals and award or withhold accreditation. The highest accreditation lasts for three years; the lowest is probationary status. The better the accreditation, the better the hospital in the eyes of the JCAH.

You may also want to read the report of the JCAH to find out what problems the hospital had at the time of the inspection. Hospitals usually know ahead of time that the JCAH is coming, so any problems that are discovered are probably persistent. If the problems raised by the JCAH concern you, ask to speak to an administrator about whether and how they have been corrected.

> **NOTE:** Dealing with such serious topics can be a very daunting experience. If you don't feel up to it, have someone you trust help you in discussing these matters with your hospital and your doctor.

—Ask your state health department if there have been any complaints about the hospital. If a patient registers a complaint about a hospital, the department may conduct an investigation. Both the complaint and the resulting report are public records that you have the right to see. And since the state department of health is unaffiliated with the JCAH, it is always a good idea to see whether the two agree on the merits or demerits of the hospital you may be thinking of entering.

—Ask your friends, relatives, doctors or medical professionals what experience they have had with the particular hospital. Learning the "word of mouth" about the hospital may be as valuable as learning what the "powers that be" think about the place. If you hear things you don't like, bring it up to your doctor and discuss it.

—Ask the administrators of the hospital if you can have a tour. The best way to check out a hotel is to inspect the place yourself. In that way you can see firsthand what the place is really like. Do the nurses seem overworked or friendly and efficient? Is the place quiet and does it appear to be clean? What are the visiting hours? Is the food any good? All of these are important since depressing surroundings aren't conducive to a prompt recovery.

—Ask the administration of several hospitals what senior services they offer and then compare. Some hospitals go out of their way to cater to the needs of senior citizens while others are seemingly indifferent and provide few "extras" for their older patients. The following is an example of a comparison of senior services available from several hospitals in a particular area. The names of the hospitals have been changed to protect the lax; the services offered have not.

Holy Cost Hospital

Free blood pressure screening

Free physician referral service

Participant in the "National Eye Care Program"

Absorbs Medicare deductible; Medicare payments accepted as payment in full

Emergency response system (see below)

Lowgrade Memorial Hospital

Free blood pressure screening

Discounts on meals purchased between 4 and 8 P.M.

Free physician referral service

Group sessions explaining Medicare benefits and supplemental insurance coverage

Ongoing efforts focusing on senior health concerns

Seniors R Us Community Hospital

House call program for seniors

Home health services for seniors

Psychological and social service support services for seniors

Full range of primary and specialty care physicians

Flu shots and other disease prevention services

Geriatric care specialists

Health insurance counseling

Health education services

Geriatric services will arrange a visit where seniors receive a free medical thermometer, a free blood glucose test and a copy of a senior survival guide

Emergency response system

Also, the availability of social workers is vital since they educate patients about outpatient community services and health care facilities.

It is obvious from these comparisons which hospital is really making a special effort to meet the special needs of seniors. You can make a similar comparison of the hospitals in your area. The results may surprise you.

You and your doctor should thoroughly discuss the medical, hotel and service functions of the hospitals in your area before you make a mutual decision as to which hospital will best serve you. For as you can see, all hospitals are not created equal.

HOME HEALTH CARE

The key words in medicine these days are "cost effective." The reality behind those words is that funding sources for health services such as Medicare and private insurance companies are working overtime to keep the cost of medical care down. As a result, the length of hospital stays is being reduced, sometimes at the expense of the patients' health. In such an atmosphere of "discharge first, ask questions later," home health care has become a necessity of life for many seniors.

What is home health care? It could be a registered nurse who makes house calls and performs services for you that a nurse in a hospital would perform such as changing dressings, administering injections or performing catheter care or it may consist of teaching you or your family to perform necessary medical services for yourselves such as the use of oxygen or insulin administration. Perhaps it is a physical therapist who helps you develop an in-home exercise program to help you regain a lost physical function. Or maybe it's hospice care that is provided (see Chapter Seven) to maximize comfort and dignity during a patient's final days. Health care is also the social services that inform you of your rights to benefits and help you and your family adjust to whatever health situation that exists.

Home health care is frequently paid for by Medicare and private health insurance. Medicaid may also pick up the tab as will workman's compensation if your medical problem is job-related.

The field is experiencing a tremendous growth so there may be several companies vying for your business, some obviously better than others. If you are in the market for home health care, here are some things to look for:

A Company Your Doctor Trusts: Most home health care is delivered with the authority of your doctor. That being the case, it only makes sense to choose a company to provide services that are known and trusted by your physician.

> **NOTE:** If you believe you would benefit from home health care and your doctor doesn't mention it, bring the subject up yourself. Doctors have been known to forget that the service is available.

A Company That Takes What Medicare Or Insurance Pays As Payment In Full: Many home health care services will "accept the assignment" and "waive the deductible" (of insurance benefits), which means you need pay nothing out of your pocket for services but merely cooperate with the processing of forms. However, all are not so accomodating so be sure you find out the company's policy regarding payment before you receive services and not after. (The Visiting Nurse Association is non-profit and partially supported by charities such as The United Way. They will often accept your case even if you have no insurance and no ability to pay.) However, there is a caveat here, which is a fancy lawyer word for warning. While Medicare and many insurance policies will pay for short-term home health care, they may not pay for long-term care. In such cases, the cost may fall on you or your family, although there may be limited help through local social welfare agencies.

A Company In Which The Service Personnel Are On Staff: Some home health care companies are more booking agents than providers of health care services. These companies contract with other companies rather than have nurses and other medical personnel on staff under their direct control. That's not to say that the services provided by such companies are poor, but there is a level of bureaucracy added between the people who hire and those who actually do the services.

A Company That Provides Training In New Techniques To Their Staff Members: Medicine is always changing and doctors are not the only ones who have to keep up with the times. Your home health care service should continually update its people. You want a company that trains its nurses and other professionals on the latest equipment.

A Company That Is Licensed: Some states license home health care agencies. While this may not be a guarantee of quality, it is better than a kick in the pants.

Home health care can truly be a godsend. At the very least, it is putting a touch of humanity back into medical care. For further information talk to your doctor, your local senior center or your Area Agency on Aging.

> **NOTE:** For more information on how to find a doctor, choose a hospital and work within the health care system, please refer to *The Doctor Book: A Nuts And Bolts Guide To Patient Power* by Wesley J. Smith (Price Stern Sloan, 1988). Sid Wolfe's book, *Worst Pills, Best Pills* is also excellent. You can get it for $12 at your local bookstore or from The Health Research Group, P.O. Box 19404, Wash., D.C. 20036

4

Double
Indemnity

Insurance And The Senior Citizen

Medicare; Medicare And HMOs; Medigap
Insurance; Medicaid; Senior Life Insurance: Long
Term (Convalescent) Care Insurance

It has been said that there are only two sure things in life, death and taxes. Well, whoever made up that saying forgot insurance. Without insurance, you cannot receive adequate medical care. Without insurance, your death can leave your family fighting off wolves at the door. Without insurance, in some states, you are not even allowed to drive a car.

Seniors already know this having spent a lifetime and a small fortune paying for insurance premiums. Having reached retirement age, senior citizens can put most of that behind them, right? Isn't that why they call this stage of life the golden years? Well, even though the chicks have left the nest and the harvest of a lifetime's work is being reaped, seniors are being sold insurance "specifically tailored" to their needs. As we shall see, some of the insurance that is being sold is quite helpful, while others are nothing more than a bill of goods.

MEDICARE

Medicare is a federal program designed to assist seniors and other eligible Americans pay their health care costs. The key word is "assist" since Medicare does not pay for all of the medical care that is received by seniors. However, if there is one insurance policy that should definitely be on every senior's insurance agenda, it is Medicare. For one thing, it is partially free. For another, it is a virtual necessity of senior life unless, of course, you like flirting with bankruptcy.

ELIGIBILITY:

In order to receive Medicare benefits you must be at least 65 and eligible to receive social security retirement benefits or be an eligible spouse. That doesn't mean you have to be actually receiving benefits. You can wait to retire and still sign up for Medicare once you hit 65. On the other hand, if you receive retirement benefits before age 65, you must wait to sign up for Medicare. The same requirements exist if you are a beneficiary of railroad retirement benefits. Those who have received social security disability benefits for two years and anyone with chronic kidney failure requiring dialysis is also eligible for benefits.

> **NOTE**: Seniors who are not eligible for Medicare may still enroll in the program if they are willing to pay a stiff premium. Contact your social security office for further details.

PART A:

Part A is a compulsory form of hospitalization insurance, paid for by social security taxes, that comes at no cost to most beneficiaries. However, a supplemental premium (a polite word for a tax) is charged to Medicare eligible seniors who pay income taxes. In 1989, the premium is $22.50 for each $150 of federal income tax paid to a maximum of $800 per enrollee. For tax years 1990, the premium will be about $37.50 per $150 of tax liability with a cap of $850. In 1991, the premium will be $39 per $150 and the cap will be $900. Thereafter—well, as the elevator operator once said, "Going up!"

Part A pays for the following:

Hospitalization. Since January 1, 1989, Medicare pays all hospitalization costs for Medicare beneficiaries after the patient pays a single annual deductible estimated at $564 (and subject to change). If you enter the hospital in December of one year, you do not have to pay the deductible for the same hospital stay if it extends into the next year.

Payments for hospitalization are made under the DRG system (Diagnosis Related Group). Under DRGs, payments are made to hospitals at a predetermined specified rate which represents the average cost of treating other patients with the same diagnosis. In other words, the hospital does not receive payments for services actually rendered to you but the predetermined amount regardless of the length of your hospital stay. The unfortunate effect of this system is to give the hospital a financial incentive to get you out of your room as soon as possible, sometimes to your health disadvantage.

Defenders of the DRG system claim that the discharge date from a hospital is to be made on the basis of the Medicare recipient's health needs alone and not on how much the hospital makes under the DRG payment. Nonetheless, there is some abuse of the system by hospitals more concerned with the bottom line than with your health. Therefore, if you believe that you or a loved one is being discharged before it is medically appropriate to do so, remember the following:

—Under the law, you do have the right to receive all of the hospital care necessary for the proper diagnosis and treatment of the illness or injury, regardless of whether or not the hospital makes a profit from your care.

—You have the right to be fully informed about decisions affecting your Medicare coverage and your medical treatment. Get these decisions in writing whenever possible, and get copies of the medical records if you believe a dispute concerning your hospitalization is likely to occur.

—You have the right to appeal written notices you receive from the hospital or Medicare stating that your hospitalization will no longer be covered. Unless the notice is in writing, there is no right to appeal, so never accept an oral statement which purports to terminate your benefits. Be sure the written notice details how an appeal is to be processed. That is your right under the law.

—If you decide to appeal, don't delay. You will be dealing with what is called a Peer Review Organization (PRO) which has the responsibility of reviewing the appropriateness and quality of hospital treatment. Upon receiving written notice of "eviction" from the hospital, call your local PRO immediately (you are covered for only two days after receiving written notice of non-coverage by the hospital). And don't leave the hospital if your doctor and you believe that such a move will adversely affect your health. Remember, if your doctor doesn't discharge you from the hospital, the hospital will have to get PRO permission to remove you, so don't be afraid to fight. If your appeal is victorious, you will continue to receive benefits for care. If not, the bill for the extra days of hospitalization will soon come in the mail.

> **NOTE**: One good reason to have your own primary care physician is that you need someone who knows you and cares enough to fight for your right to receive individualized care.

Skilled Nursing: If you need inpatient skilled nursing care after hospitalization, Part A will help pay for up to 150 days worth of care. The first eight days are subject to a 20% co-payment of approximately $21 per day. Thereafter, the government picks up the rest of the tab until your time of coverage has expired.

Home Health Care: As discussed in the last chapter, home health care is a vital part of today's senior health care system. Medicare will pay for a Medicare certified agency to provide medically necessary part-time skilled nursing, physical therapy or speech therapy. If you receive any of these services you may also be eligible for part-time home health aides, medical and social services and supplies. The bad news is that Medicare will not foot the bill for full-time nursing care at home, meals or housekeeping services. However, when Medicare does pay, it pays in full.

Hospice Care: Medicare recipients who have been diagnosed as having a terminal illness can qualify for hospice care during the latter part of their ordeal. There is no maximum amount of time that can be covered, so long as the beneficiary is certified every 210 days as terminally ill. Covered services under hospice care include: doctors' services, nursing services, medical appliances, outpatient drugs for pain relief, home health aide, homemaker services, therapies, medical social services and short periods of inpatient care whether for medical or respite (caregiver time off) purposes. Counseling for the patient and family are also included. Except for medications and respite care, Medicare pays 100% of the cost of services rendered.

PART B:

Medicare Part B is a voluntary major medical health insurance plan that is not free but costs a modest amount per month which is usually deducted from your social security check. Part B helps pay for doctors' services, outpatient hospital care, outpatient surgery, ambulance services, professionally administered medication (as opposed to self-administered medicines), a large percentage of other prescribed medications after you have paid the first $600 (beginning in 1991) and the cost of certain medical equipment and supplies. Some types of oral surgery can also be covered as well as outpatient physical therapy and speech therapy. Home health care is also covered if ordered by your doctor.

Unfortunately, Medicare will not pay for many preventative care measures such as regular and routine checkups, screening tests and inoculations. However, there are exceptions. For example, shots to prevent pneumococcal infection are already covered, and beginning in 1991, preventative mammogram screenings will be partially paid for by Medicare. However, if the physical examination or tests are conducted as part of an attempt at diagnosing the cause of symptoms or a malady as opposed to a preventative measure, they are covered assuming the exams or tests are deemed "medically necessary" (see below) by Medicare. Be sure to discuss with your doctor whether your tests or physical examination will be covered by Medicare before you receive them.

Here's how Part B works:

—Payments to physicians are based on what is called a "reasonable charge" for the service performed. For example, let's say that you came to your doctor complaining of feeling tired all of the time. Your doctor examined you and took blood tests and found that you suffered from a disease that can be promptly treated and cured. Even if your doctor charged you $1,000 for these services, Medicare only reimburses what they consider to be a reasonable charge for the doctor's services. This amount is almost always less than the actual charge. You may be the one who has to pay the difference between the actual charge and Medicare's determination of reasonable charge.

—Whether or not you have to pay the difference is determined by which doctor you choose. A doctor who "accepts the assignment" is paid directly by Medicare as is stipulated under Part B. In return for receiving these direct payments, the doctor agrees to accept whatever Medicare determines is a reasonable charge for the services that were rendered. For instance, if the doctor charges $1,000 and Medicare deems the service to be worth $750, the doctor accepts the $750 determination as his or her full charge for services rendered.

—If your doctor does not "accept the assignment," you must pay your doctor his or her actual charges, and you are reimbursed directly by Medicare for its share of what it deems to be the reasonable charge. Again referring to our example, you pay the doctor the full $1000 but are reimbursed based on a fee of $750. By using a doctor that does not "accept the assignment," you are vastly increasing the cost of your medical care.

> **NOTE:** Medicare publishes a list of many of the doctors willing to accept the assignment in your area. These doctors are called Medicare Participating Physicians and the list is called the Medicare Participating Physician/Supplier Directory. It is available through most local senior citizen organizations.

—Medicare will pay 80% of the reasonable charge less a deductible which is currently $75 per year. Assuming you have paid the deductible, here is how the $1,000 charge would be handled by both a doctor who does and a doctor who does not accept the assignment.

	M.D. ACCEPTS ASSIGNMENT	M.D. DOES NOT ACCEPT ASSIGNMENT
M.D.'s Actual Charge	$1,000	$1,000
Reasonable Charge Allowed by Medicare	$750	$750
Medicare Pays M.D. (80% of $750)	$600	N/A
Medicare Pays Patient (80% OF $750)	N/A	$600
What Patient Pays	$150 ($750 Reasonable Cost Minus $600 Reimbursed Patient by Medicare)	$400 ($1,000 Actual Cost Minus $600 Paid M.D. by Medicare)

Medicare also reserves the right to judge whether a performed service is "medically necessary." If, upon receiving your claim, it is determined that you didn't need the service after all, they will deny the claim forcing you to appeal or pay the doctor yourself (probably both since most appeals are denied.)

As of January 1, 1990, there will be a cap on out-of-pocket Part B expenses to be paid by benificiaries of $1,370 after which Medicare will pay 100% of all covered services. As with other Medicare expenses, the cap will be raised annually. However, remember, there is a difference between a reasonable charge and an actual charge, so even if Medicare is paying 100% and you have a doctor that does not accept the assignment, you may still have to make up the difference between the actual charge and the amount Medicare pays.

Beginning January 1, 1990, Medicare will pay for respite care up to 80 hours per year to give respite to unpaid family members or an unpaid friend who lives with and cares for a chronically dependent Medicare beneficiary. Such respite care could include homemaking duties, personal care or nursing care. To be eligible, a benificiary would have to meet the following requirements:

1) Be unable for at least three months to perform two or

more "activities of daily living" including eating, dressing, bathing, toileting or moving into or out of bed.

2) Have incurred medical expenses high enough to have exceeded either the Medicare prescription-deductible or the Part B out-of-pocket cap.

There may be a co-insurance payment owed for respite care depending on individual circumstances.

Beginning in 1991, Medicare will pay for a portion of prescription drugs after a $600 deductible. Medicare will also create a "participating pharmacy program" similar to the participating physician program described earlier. Participating pharmacies will, among other things, be prevented from charging more for prescription drugs than Medicare.

For more details on Medicare, contact your local social security office or buy a copy of the very detailed book *Social Security, Medicare And Pensions*, (Nolo Press, 950 Parker Street, Berkeley, CA 94710, $14.95).

MEDICARE AND HMOs:

The new kid on the health insurance block is the HMO (Health Maintenance Organization). The concept of the HMO is simple; you pay the insurance premiums and the HMO provides you with all of your medical care. There is a catch, of course. You must restrict your medical care to doctors and medical facilities authorized by the plan except in life threatening emergencies. In other words, you lose your freedom of choice.

Today, many HMOs are actively soliciting business from Medicare recipients. Those who wish to join an HMO give up their rights under Medicare. You will also probably have to give up your current doctor. In return, Medicare pays the HMO for your membership in the program. Once a member, the former Medicare recipient must receive benefits which, at minimum, equal those that would have been obtained under Medicare.

If you are interested in the HMO concept, be sure to shop around because the plans that are offered to Medicare recipients vary greatly. For example, some plans may require the new HMO member to pay co-payments similar to those paid under Medicare while others offer care virtually free of charge. Some plans have a large number of doctors to choose from while others do not. Still others may offer services above and beyond those available under Medicare while others offer the lowest level of services legally permissable to Medicare approved plans.

If you are going to join an HMO, ask the following questions of the plan administrators before you give up your Medicare benefits.

What emphasis does the HMO give to geriatrics? HMOs usually seek to achieve a broad base of plan members from throughout the community. This may not bode well for you as a senior citizen since the medical needs of seniors may be far different from those of younger persons. If you do decide to give up your freedom to choose any doctor in the community who accepts Medicare patients, it is a good idea to make sure that the plan has doctors available to you who enjoy tending to the needs of older people and who keep current on the changing geriatric medical scene.

What does the HMO offer that I can't get from Medicare? If you are going to give up freedom of choice, you should at least be given something in return. This should mean extra services, such as free preventative care or free medicine.

What is the most I will have to pay per year? Again, you should receive a quid pro quo for what you give up when you join an HMO through Medicare. This should be a lower worst-case financial risk. Even though you give up Medicare benefits, you still must pay for Part B, so be sure to include those costs in your estimate.

What hospitals does the plan use? Remember what we said about all hospitals not being created equal? This truth is not blunted because the hospitalization is provided through an HMO. Thus a big issue in your decision regarding an HMO should be the quality of the hospitals that are utilized by the plan.

How many sub-specialists are approved by the plan? Most HMOs have a large number of primary care physicians from which to choose. However, when it comes to specialists, the choices may be quite limited. So, this question may be very important to you, especially if you are already seeing a specialist whom you may have to give up when you join the HMO.

What is the grievance procedure? When you join an HMO, you do not give up your Medicare grievance procedures. Ideally, however, any problems that arise can be resolved between the plan and yourself. The easier the grievance procedure, the more likely you will be to stand up for your rights.

MEDIGAP POLICIES

As can be seen from the discussion above, there are wide gaps in the protection Medicare affords. These gaps come in two basic types: coverage gaps and benefits gaps. The term "coverage gap" refers to medical services that Medicare doesn't pay for such as eyeglasses and dentures and, most importantly, long-term nursing home care. The term "benefits gap" deals with items for which Medicare pays only partial benefits. The deductible and the 80% cap on benefits under Part B are just two examples.

A boom industry in the insurance field has grown around insurance policies that protect its beneficiaries from benefit gaps. (With the exception of nursing home insurance that will be discussed below, very few policies provide protection for coverage gaps.) These policies, popularly known as "medigap" policies can be an important defense against health care costs. They can also be a waste of money if the wrong policy is selected.

WHO NEEDS A MEDI-GAP POLICY?

In a way, people who get hit the worst by Medicare benefit gaps are the same people who get hit the hardest by taxes; in other words the middle class. That's because the rich can pay the gap without a problem, and the poor can probably qualify for Medicaid (see below) which will fill most gaps. But the vast middle class—ah yes, they get it in the neck again.

However, even members of the middle class can sometimes avoid the extra expense of such insurance policies or the risk of opting to rely on Medicare alone. For example, some companies and unions provide continued health insurance upon retirement. Check your insurance policy. You may find that you are already covered. Those who work may have health insurance provided as a benefit of employment. Medicare recipients who join HMOs may also not need such policies if the plan benefits are halfway decent.

TIPS ON BUYING MEDI-GAP POLICIES:

If you are interested in Medi-gap policies, here are some tips to help find the right policy for you:

Compare Several Policies Before Buying: Before you buy, get what is called an "outline of coverage" from several plans. These outlines are basically spreadsheets, and by comparing and contrasting several, you should be able to get a good idea of the benefits provided versus the cost of each policy so you can get the most protection your budget can afford.

Here is an example of what I mean. The following is an actual comparison from the California Department of Insurance of actual policies available in that state. As you will see, prices and services vary widely. Also, remember, that these policies may not be the same ones as those available to you.

POLICY	A	B	C	D	E
Part A deductible covered?	no	no	yes	yes	yes
Part B deductible covered?	no	no	no	no	yes
Part B additional deductible covered?	yes	no	yes	yes	yes
Part B expenses in excess of $5000 covered?	yes	no	yes	yes	yes
Coverage for difference in reasonable charge and charge of doctor?	no	no	no	30%	after 1st $200
Skilled nursing facility covered?	no	no	medicare co-payment from 100th through 365th day	co-payment through 100th day	through 100th day
Other benefits	none	none	limited private duty nurse	none	none
Premium at age 70 (yearly)	$215.40	$207	$450-$567	$789 (male) $684 (female)	$711 male $606 female
Comments			group plan only		

As you can see, there are differences between each policy with those having better coverage costing more to purchase.

—Don't listen to an agent who tells you that the policy will cover every expense not paid by Medicare. Such policies do not exist.

—Don't be pressured by scare tactics into purchasing. One such tactic is to terrify you about the high cost of hospitalization after Medicare stops paying. That part is true, but what the agent might not tell you is that the average hospital stay is approximately one week which is paid by Medicare.

—Don't buy multiple policies. You will just be duplicating basic benefits.

—Don't pay cash for a policy. Write a check to the company, not the agent.

—Don't believe any agent who tells you that his or her company is affiliated with the government. Such companies do not exist.

—If you are changing policies, be sure to keep your old one until your new one takes full effect, including any waiting periods and pre-existing condition exclusions (see below).

—Be sure to read the fine print. Many policies have benefits that may not live up to your expectations or the sales agent's hype.

Pre-existing illness exclusions: Many policies exclude prior illnesses or conditions for which you have recently been treated from coverage either for the duration of the policy or for a specific period of time after the policy goes into effect. Let's say you suffer from cancer and had a course of radiation treatment three months prior to your purchase of the policy. If there is a pre-existing illness exclusion clause, and you need further treatment, your policy would not be there to help you bail water out of your leaky financial boat.

Indemnity payments: An indemnity benefit pays a specific amount of money for each day hospitalized. The amount is fixed and will not rise with the increasing prices for medical care, so inflation can eat into the "benefit of the benefit" pretty quickly. Some indemnity plans also deduct from the benefits owed an amount equivalent to that paid by Medicare thereby severely reducing the benefit that is paid.

Elimination periods: Here's a little trick that some indemnity policies pull. Rather than pay you your daily benefit from day one in the hospital, they will have an "elimination period" which you must go through before benefits are paid. This elimination period can be up to a week. Remember what we said about the DRG payment system? One effect of this reform has been to reduce the length of average hospitalization for Medicare benificiaries. If the elimination period is a long one, chances are you may never see the cash you were promised when you signed up for the policy.

Co-payment plans: Co-payment plans only pay the 20% of the reasonable charge as determined by Medicare. In other words, if your doctor does not accept the assignment, the money paid by the insurance company will not be 20% of the cost of your care at all, but a lower percentage depending upon how much higher the actual charge was over the reasonable charge.

Renewability clauses: You want a medi-gap policy that guarantees your right to renew the policy for life. Remember, you are dealing with an insurance company here and despite their advertising promos about being caring companies who should be considered as part of the family, they are in business to make money. Give them a loophole which allows them to stop covering you if you have become ill, and they'll drive an 18 wheel truck right through it. Do not sign up for a policy that is "optionally renewable," which means the company can decline to renew at the end of the policy year if it so desires.

If you are not signed up for Medicare, you do not want a medi-gap policy but some form of other traditional health insurance plan. If you retire before the age of 65 and have a good health insurance plan available as a benefit of employment, be sure to see whether your company or union offers a "conversion policy" to hold you until you are eligible for Medicare, or see if you can obtain independent health insurance coverage. For a full discussion of the various types of health insurance plans offered on the market, please refer to *The Doctor Book: A Nuts and Bolts Guide to Patient Power* (Price Stern Sloan, 1988) by Wesley J. Smith.

MEDICAID

Medicaid is a federally assisted, state administered health care program which assists the poor who are aged, blind, disabled or have dependent children. All states except Arizona participate in the plan, although Arizona has a similar plan of its own. The name of the Medicaid plan will vary from state to state.

Since the funding for each state's program is partially state supplied and each state differs on what they can afford to pay, how much recipients pay and the range of medical services available may vary. However, the following programs are offered to Medicaid recipients:

—Inpatient and outpatient hospital services
—Lab and X-ray services
—Skilled nursing care at home, if necessary
—Physicians' services

Some plans also pay for eyeglasses, prescription drugs and intermediate health care facilities.

To be eligible, you have to be in significant financial need. For older people who are being eaten alive by medical bills, this can mean the loss of a lifetime's savings and the sale of much of their property before they can find some Medicaid relief since some states are even stricter than SSI in determining eligibility. However, many states ease this burden by allowing needy persons to qualify under the "medically needy" formula. This formula allows an applicant to subtract medical bills from his or her income and assets, thus allowing otherwise ineligible applicants to qualify for benefits without having to actually move to the poor farm. (Contact your state Medicaid office for the details in your area.)

The applicant's income and that of his or her spouse is usually counted in determining eligibility (with some exceptions, such as if one spouse is in a nursing home or if the parties are separated.) If the applicant is living with a child or relative, that person's assets are not counted. However, if a child or relative financially supports the applicant, the amount of support will be considered in determining whether he or she can be signed up for the program.

> **NOTE:** Not all physicians or medical facilities are willing to treat Medicaid recipients. To find who will in your locality, contact your state or local health department which will also be able to give you detailed information on eligibility requirements in your state.

SENIOR LIFE INSURANCE

Most seniors are familiar with the type of life insurance policy whereby the insurance company is betting that you live, and you are betting that you die. If you live, they collect premiums and pay you nothing (except under "whole life" policies where you build up an equity in your policy). If you die, the life insurance company pays your benificiaries the face amount of the life insurance policy.

Life insurance has traditionally been purchased as a way of protecting the family in the event of the death of the breadwinner(s). However, by the time they reach retirement age, many seniors either no longer have policies, or they have long since cashed them in since their children now have children of their own as well as their own life insurance policies.

Most life insurance companies don't want the business of seniors since the risk of death is greater for a 70 year old than a 30 year old. However, there are some companies that market specifically to seniors and appeal to their familiarity with life insurance protection. These companies usually have a famous actor as their spokesman and they usually guarantee that "you cannot be turned down for any reason." While they offer a deal too good for you to turn down, a close analysis of their benefits leaves much to be desired.

Here is a comparison of the claim and the actual benefit or

term of a typical company taken directly from their sales brochure:

CLAIM: Affordable term life insurance as little as $3.95 per month.

TERM: If you are a man, the $3.95 would only pay $600 for your death by natural causes if you die at age 64 and just $400 for if you die between the ages of 70-74. If you die because of an accident at age 70, the benefit would only be $3,280, barely enough to pay for a decent burial. In order for a 70 year old man to receive a natural death benefit of only $1,400, he would have to pay a premium of $19.75 per month. Benefits are slightly higher for women. If a husband and wife both age 70-74 want to be covered for $1,400 and $2,000 respectively, the premium would be almost $40 dollars a month or $480 per year!

CLAIM: No medical exam required; no questions asked!

TERM: They can offer this "benefit" because if you die of natural causes in the first two years, the only benefit you will receive is a return of your premiums.

CLAIM: Up to $44,400 in total benefits, depending on age and sex.

TERM: The key words are "total benefits" since there is a distinction between natural death and accidental death. In order to receive big bucks upon a death, the death must be accidental. The only person who could qualify for $44,400 is a woman age 40-44 who spent $19.95 per month on the policy and who dies an accidental death. A natural death would only pay $9,600. A woman paying the same premium who dies accidentally at age 68 would receive $21, 800. However, if she dies of natural causes, she would only receive $3,000! There's another catch. An exclusion under the accidental death benefit is made for accidents resulting "directly or indirectly from: any disease or bodily infirmity. . . ." In other words, if you fall down a flight of stairs because you are old or sick, your beneficiaries might not be able to collect the larger accidental death benefit.

I'm not saying you shouldn't buy this type of policy, but please read the brochure carefully in order to see what you are really getting for your money. You may just decide the price isn't worth the benefit.

LONG-TERM CARE INSURANCE

One of the tragedies of modern senior life is the fact that Medicare and Medi-gap policies do not, at present, pay for long-term nursing home care. In fact, unless and until the patient is practically pauperized and can qualify for Medicaid, it is almost impossible to receive any governmental assistance whatsoever.

This is unfortunate because long-term care is very expensive. According to the Health Insurance Association of America, the average yearly cost of such nursing home care came to about $2,000 a month!

There is a relatively new insurance policy on the market called long-term care insurance or nursing home insurance which is designed to pay benefits if the beneficiary must enter a nursing home.

If you are interested in looking into nursing home insurance, Helen Abbott of Phoenix, Arizona, an independent insurance agent who specializes in insurance policies for senior citizens, advises that you look for and understand the following concerning any policy you purchase:

Guaranteed Renewability: This means if you pay your premiums on time, the insurer can't refuse to renew.

Pre-existing Conditions Clause: Most policies have a waiting period before your pre-existing conditions will be covered if at all. The average waiting period is six months after the date your policy becomes effective.

Levels of Care: All levels of care, whether skilled, intermediate or custodial, should be paid a FULL benefit for the ENTIRE length of time. Older policies stated you had to receive skilled care from one to twenty days before the insurance would cover intermediate or custodial care. But some of the newer policies will now pay benefits regardless of the level of care into which you were admitted.

Mental Diseases: Be certain that Alzheimer's Disease, senility dementia and other organic mental conditions are covered. Some policies exclude all mental diseases. Check the policy's "exclusion clause" and "outline coverage" sections to see how this is treated.

Prior Hospital Confinement: Most long-term care policies require prior hospitalization, usually three days. There are a few plans on the market that don't insist on this, but they charge a higher premium. (This is one aspect of nursing home insurance policies that really riled the good folks at Consumers Union. They contend that around 60% of all nursing home patients enter the facilities without being hospitalized beforehand. That means that if that 60% had insurance requiring prior hospitalization, those people would receive no benefits whatsoever from their insurance policies.)

Deductible Periods: When does the policy actually start paying? Most common is the 20-day deductible. This means the insurance company begins paying benefits on the 21st day of confinement in a nursing home.

Permanent Age: Be sure that the age at which you take out

the policy is the age at which your premiums will be computed for the life of the policy.

Inflation Fighter: Most policies are indemnity policies which means that they pay a fixed amount of benefit per day which does not go up with inflation.

Right to Return: If, for whatever reason, you are not satisfied with the policy, you have the right to return it for a refund of the total premium within ten days of receiving the policy.

Waiver of Premium: If you are receiving benefits for a period of time, the company will pay your premiums for the remainder of your covered confinements.

An A + Insurance Company: You don't want an insurance company that is here today when you pay your premium and gone tomorrow when you file your claim. That's why it is always a good idea to pick a nationally recognized company or at least one that has a good reputation with your state department of insurance.

(Reprinted with the permission of Helen Abbott)

The market is quickly evolving with new companies and policies coming on the market every day. However, just because the field is relatively new doesn't mean that it's not controversial. Consumers Union stated in a 1988 press release that the premiums for these policies are either too expensive (running between $100 and $260 a month) for most people or not worth it for those with limited means since they would quickly become eligible for Medicaid. They further contend that the private sector is simply not up to solving the problem of long-term care. Naturally, the insurance industry disagrees; they believe that competition will make policies more affordable and more helpful to beneficiaries. Who's right? Well, in a free country, the answer to that question is up to you.

5

Getting The Most Out Of Life

Strategies For Active Living

Volunteerism; Action Agency; Retired Senior Volunteer Program; Senior Companion; Foster Grandparents; Peace Corps; Self-Improvement; Elderhostel; Travel Tips; Senior Centers

If Cicero was right when he said, "Old age, the crown of life, our play's last act," then the senior years should be the most interesting time of all. In the United States, that sentiment may be easier said than done. While many cultures revere their elderly, we tend to worship the ideal of youth. Many seem to think that old people have nothing to offer.

Don't you believe it! Now more than ever, seniors have the opportunity to lead rich, productive lives, full of meaning and service, lives of thrills and adventure, contentment and joy. Today opportunities abound to make the last act the best act. And when the time comes to take that curtain call in the sky, how fine it will be to know that you left them wanting more.

VOLUNTEERISM

The word "volunteer" comes from French and means "one who enters into a service of his or her own free will." That definition does not mean that the volunteer receives nothing in return. After all, the bible says, "As ye shall sow, so shall ye reap." In the eastern religions, they call this concept karma. In our times we say what goes around comes around, or you receive from life exactly what you put into it. Maybe that's why volunteers seem unusually fulfilled and happy.

The importance of volunteerism goes beyond personal satisfaction. It is, in fact, one of our most important national resources and has been since the founding of the republic. In the early 1800s, a Frenchman named Alexis de Tocqueville said about the subject, "The spirit of neighbor helping neighbor is what distinguishes America's national character." It was true then and it remains true today.

ACTION AGENCIES:

The federal government has recognized this fact and has created ACTION, a federal agency that promotes volunteerism. Action volunteers help alleviate poverty, teach the illiterate, combat drug abuse, work to prevent crime, supplement community social services, offer counsel to the troubled and generally provide hundreds of different types of volunteer services throughout the country.

Of the many volunteer programs offered by ACTION, three are designed specifically with seniors in mind: the Retired Senior Volunteer Program (RSVP), the Senior Companion Program and the Foster Grandparent Program. Here's the scoop on all three:

RSVP:

Repondez s'il vous plait is French for please respond— and respond seniors do, 365,000 of them, to their country's call for volunteers under the RSVP program. RSVP was launched in 1971 as a bold response to the realities of an aging America. The idea is quite simple: harness the power and skills of seniors who have left the work force and focus that energy into community service and the nonprofit sector for the purpose of bettering American communities and the lives of the volunteers.

The ingredients that make RSVP such a vital force is local administration and local support. While most of the money to operate the program is generated on the federal level, the responsibility for running the show falls on local chapters called volunteer stations. This means that volunteers are able to be directed to the areas of greatest community need. Station staff members work hard to develop volunteer opportunities, match these needs to the volunteer talent available, provide pre-service orientation and training and arrange matters of transportation and meals for volunteers where possible.

Since each station responds to the needs of its locality, the type of work that is offered will vary from place to place. However, volunteers generally work in the following fields:

Service To The Next Generation: Kids today need help to resist drugs, gangs and illiteracy. RSVP is right there providing a helping hand in literacy training, support for abused children and crisis intervention for problems related to teen pregnancy and runaways. A prime example of the old helping the young is Kindergarden Intervention in Los Angeles where RSVP volunteers work one-on-one with disturbed kindergartners to prevent today's unhappy child from becoming tomorrow's high school dropout. One changed life can create a ripple effect on the child's peers and eventual offspring. That's work that lasts more than a lifetime.

Community Support: RSVP volunteers can be found in hospitals, blood banks, libraries, food cooperatives, food banks and crop recovery programs. The list is as endless as the need.

Helping Those Who Can't Help Themselves: Many housebound elderly and sick people's lives would be made even more difficult without RSVP volunteers who provide homemaker services, respite care, personal care and escorting, shopping and recreational assistance for those unable to provide these services to themselves. With government funds for such needed activities shrinking, the need for volunteers to fill the vacuum grows every year.

Crime Prevention: If you think we've got a crime problem now, imagine how much worse it might be if more than 64 million hours of service in one year alone were not donated by RSVP volunteers to help prevent crime. Have you heard of fraud prevention education? RSVP is there. Does your neighborhood need crime prevention and reporting skills taught to its elderly residents? RSVP does the job. Citizen patrols? RSVP works there, too. If the crime prevention activity is appropriate for non-uniformed personnel to perform, chances are there is an opportunity for an RSVP volunteer there.

Too many people never experience the joy and personal satisfaction of working with RSVP. They don't feel they have anything to contribute. This seems especially true of women who may be widowed or divorced and who spent their youth and middle age raising a family. "What can I do?" they ask. "I have no skills. I didn't work. I was just a housewife." Althea Ludowitz, Director of an RSVP Station, hears that plaintive cry all of the time. Her answer:

> "Those 'just housewives' have so many talents. If they've raised a family and managed to get the children dressed and out of the house and off to school, get a husband off to work, do the marketing, buy the clothing—they have so many skills that are so very useful—and for years they have been told they're 'just a housewife.' The first thing I say is, 'Now wait a minute, you're not just a housewife, you're a home manager and you have a whole lot of skills to offer to people and agencies. They may have less than a

high school education, but they still have skills and we delight in putting them right to work in everything from folding and stuffing envelopes to working closely with people from all ages and backgrounds."

Your community needs YOU. Regardless of your skills or education RSVP has a job that's just right for you.

Senior Companion Program: The Senior Companion Program manages to kill two birds with one stone. The "birds" are poverty and helplessness. The stone is the Senior Companion Program which pays low income seniors (age 60 and above who are in relatively good health) to nourish and care for their compatriots who find it difficult to do for themselves.

Senior Companions work 20 hours per week and as their name implies, they literally become the companion of a fellow senior. They do perform all kinds of services including letter writing, running errands, light housekeeping and most important, companionship. They receive a stipend of somewhat over two dollars per hour, a meal, transportation costs and accident insurance to cover them while they perform their services. They also receive a free physical annually. And the satisfaction? It's unlimited.

Those needing assistance can reach the Companion program through their local Action Program or Senior Companion Station. There is no charge for the service and no qualifications other than being over 60 with a need to fill.

Foster Grandparent Program: The flip side of the Senior Companion program is the Foster Grandparent program. Foster Grandparents work four hours a day, five days per week assisting "special" children adjust to life. Children afflicted with Down's Syndrome, blindness, cerebral palsy or who are disturbed or in detention, are given life's most precious gift, unconditional love, by their volunteer grandparents.

As with the Senior Companion Program, Foster Grand-parents must be at least 60, in reasonably good health and very full of heart. A stipend is paid for the work and a meal provided as well as transportation, an annual physical and insurance.

If you are interested in becoming a Foster Grandparent, contact your local Action Agency. But watch out. I'm told that once a volunteer participates in the program, they're hooked for life.

If you are interested in further information about these or other Action Volunteer Programs such as Volunteers in Service to America (VISTA) contact your local Action Agency or one of the following Regional Offices:

Region I— 10 Causeway Street, Room 473
Boston, Mass. 02222-1039
Phone—(617) 565-7001
(Vermont, New Hampshire, Rhode Island, Maine, Massachusetts and Connecticut)

Region II— Jacob K. Javits Fed. Bldg.
26 Federal Plaza, Suite 1611
New York, N.Y. 10278
Phone—(212) 264-4747
(New York, New Jersey, Puerto Rico and the Virgin Islands)

Region III—U.S. Customs House, Room 108
2nd and Chestnut Streets
Philadelphia, PA. 19106
Phone—(215) 597-9972
(Pennsylvania, Delaware, Maryland, Virginia, West Virginia and the District of Columbia)

Region IV— 101 Marietta ST. N.W., Suite 1003
Atlanta, GA. 30323

Phone—(404) 331-2859
(Georgia, Florida, Alabama, North Carolina, Kentucky, Mississippi, Tennessee and South Carolina)

Region V— 10 West Jackson Blvd.
Chicago, IL. 60604
Phone—(312) 353-5107
(Minnesota, Wisconsin, Michigan, Illinois, Indiana and Ohio)

Region VI— Federal Building, Room 6B11
1100 Commerce St.
Dallas TX. 75242.
Phone—(214) 767-9494
(New Mexico, Oklahoma, Texas, Arkansas, and Louisiana)

Region VII— Two Gateway Center
4th and State St. Room 330
Kansas City, KS. 66101
Phone—(913) 758-4472
(Nebraska, Iowa, Kansas and Missouri)

Region VIII—Executive Tower Building, Suite 2930
1405 Curtis St. Denver, CO. 80202
Phone—(303) 844-2671
(Montana, North Dakota, Colorado, South Dakota, Utah and Wyoming)

Region IX— 211 Main St., Room 530
San Fransisco, CA. 94105
Phone—(415) 974-0673
(California, Nevada, Arizona, Hawaii, Guam and American Samoa)

Region X—Federal Office Bldg., Suite 3039
       909 First Ave., Seattle, WA. 98174
       Phone—(206) 442-1558
       (Washington, Oregon, Idaho and Alaska)

THE PEACE CORPS:

Seniors, Uncle Sam, wearing his Peace Corps' hat, definitely wants YOU! He wants you in Barbados helping farmers plan irrigation systems. He wants you in Paraguay helping to design warehouses and flood control systems. He wants you in Nepal teaching math in a village school high in the Himalayas. He wants you in Mali, West Africa, planning nutrition programs. He wants you anywhere in the world that Americans can safely go and make a difference to people who need our help.

But why older Americans? Aren't younger people better for the job? Not according to Charna R. Lefton, a Public Affairs Manager for the Corps, who told me, "In most developing nations, their culture is such that age is something that is respected and their experience is looked upon as giving them a great deal of wisdom and knowledge that only comes from living. In fact, older Americans tend to get extra respect because of their age."

There are really very few requirements to volunteer for the Peace Corps. You must be a citizen of the United States. You must also be able to meet certain medical requirements, but these standards are no problem for older Americans in relatively good health. There may be a requirement that you possess certain skills or experience, usually the equivalent of a four year degree or three to five years work experience. But that's about it. There is no upper age limit!

Volunteering in the Peace Corps is simply taking your years of experience and putting it to work for others in the hope of promoting prosperity and world peace. If your background is in agriculture, your skills are needed to work in crop development, plant protection, agricultural education, beekeeping and animal husbandry. If you have a skilled trade, you are needed to pass your gifts on to others. If you can teach, the Peace Corps can turn you onto some very hungry and appreciative minds. Whatever your background, the Peace Corps needs you.

Volunteers receive much in return for that which they give. First, there are the intangibles such as the feeling of making a difference and the satisfaction of a job well done. Then, there is the adventure of it all, literally a once in a lifetime experience. In addition, volunteers receive $175 for each month of training and service. That works out to $4,200 for a two year assignment. That means that if you are on social security or retirement pay, you can bank your checks while in the Corps and come home to quite a nice little pot o' gold. Many use the opportunity of being overseas to travel after their service is up before taking their free plane ride home.

While in service, you will receive language training, good health care, technical training, cross-cultural training and vacation time which accrues at two days per month. Communication is allowed with family and loved ones who can write (although the mail is slow—even by post office standards). They are also allowed to visit at their expense. In an emergency, the Peace Corps will fly you home for up to two weeks and then back to your assignment at no expense to you.

If you would like more information of the Peace Corp or an application to join up, call toll free (800) 424-8580 ext. 93 or contact:

The Peace Corps
Room P-301
Washington D.C. 20526

Service Corps Of Retired Executives: If you are a retired business executive who would like to use the business skills honed during your career to help strengthen the free enterprise system, you can do so by volunteering to aid owners of small businesses or community groups in need of management assistance. The Service Corps of Retired Executives (SCORE) in conjunction with the Small Business Administration puts retired business persons in touch with those who need their business savvy to make things run smoothly and efficiently. If that appeals to you, contact your local Action office or office of the Small Business Administration. There is no salary, but expenses are paid. And as for company benefits, well, if job satisfaction is a benefit, you'll be one of the best compensated people in your community.

UNITED WAY VOLUNTEER BUREAUS:

In addition to national programs, there are plenty of state and local volunteer opportunities, some run by government entities, others by the countless agencies in the nonprofit sector. With so many volunteer opportunities available, it is easy to lose the forest for the trees. That's where the United Way comes in. The United Way has local "Volunteer Bureaus" that refer volunteers to the opportunities in each locale.

A typical volunteer bureau exists in Maricopa County, Arizona in the Phoenix area. The bureau publishes a booklet called the Volunteer Directory which lists most, if not all, agencies looking for assistance. The fields requesting help range from law to medicine to job training to recreation to aiding the retarded. In addition to the "expected" requests such as the American Red Cross and hospitals, the directory lists opportunities in children's homes, an art commission, libraries, a public television station and the Special Olympics, just to name five out of 282 listings requesting volunteers.

If you want to help, but can't find the right volunteer glove size to wear, contact your local United Way. They have more than enough jobs for you!

AARP VOLUNTEER PROGRAMS:

The AARP also runs many very worthwhile volunteer programs. For example, "Health Care Volunteers in Action" makes extensive use of volunteers to accomplish three goals:
—making health care more affordable;
—improving the quality and access to care;
—helping older people to develop healthier life styles.

Volunteers in this program conduct pharmacy price surveys, counsel older people on their rights under Medicare and Medicaid, act as consumer advocates for patients in nursing homes, help the AARP lobby legislators regarding health care legislation and much more all aimed at helping older Americans live as healthily as possible.

"Reminiscence" is another program in which volunteers are trained to employ their listening and visiting skills in sharing another person's cherished memories, a service of great importance to the many homebound and shut-ins who suffer from loss of contact with family and friends.

If you would like more information on how you can make a difference hand in hand with the AARP, write to:

AARP Program Department
1909 K Street N.W.
Washington D.C. 20049

SELF-IMPROVEMENT

We are never too old to learn and grow. This is especially true in the retirement years when many have the first opportunity of their adult lives to pursue the things that interest them. For some, self-improvement merely means working on that golf game in order to break into the low eighties. For others, it is going back to school to get that long-delayed high school diploma or college degree. Maybe you always wanted to build a dream home from scratch in the Florida everglades. There are as many ways to improve self as there are selves to be improved.

There is a program out there in retirement land that many find very exciting. This program is called Elderhostel, and it consists of a network of over 1,000 colleges, universities and other educational institutions which offer low-cost, short-term, residential academic programs for older adults. It is a wonderful and imaginative twist of the "youth hostels" concept of European fame.

Most Elderhostel programs last for one week and offer up to three specially designed courses in the liberal arts. The hostelers, as the program participants are called, also take part in extracurricular activities such as cultural and social events that add to the fun. Elderhostel provides an informal atmosphere where making new friends is easy, and the educational program is stimulating.

There are Elderhostel opportunities in every state, Canada and at least 30 other countries around the world. Courses run the gamut and include: photography, current issues in foreign policy, Quakerism, crime fiction, the big band era and teaching chimps sign language. There are literally hundreds of courses to choose from.

Anyone age 60 and above, or the spouse or companion of an attending hosteler age 60 and above may attend. While enrolled in the courses selected, you stay in the dorms of the participating institution and eat in the campus cafeteria along with 20-40 other Elderhostel classmates. The cost is reasonable, running from about $200 for room and board, classes, use of school facilities and extracurricular activities for the week. The overseas programs are more expensive and usually run three weeks longer. Transportation is not included. There are a number of "hostelships" available for those who may not be able to afford the full cost of the program.

For more information about the program, contact:

Elderhostel
80 Boylston Street, Suite 400
Boston, Massachusetts 02116

TRAVEL

One of the joys of life for many retired seniors is the opportunity to travel and visit long lost relatives and friends. Many want to see exotic places and others simply want the sun in their faces and the wind at their back. Whether you are traveling across the street or around the world, here are some tips to make your experience safe and joyful:

Use the services of a travel agent: Travel agents earn their living by booking the business and pleasure travel plans of their clients with the airlines, hotels, cruise lines, tour packagers and others who provide travel services. There are several reasons to use a reputable travel agent to assist you in your travel plans.

Free service: The agent's commission is paid by the enterprise whose travel services you buy and not by you. As far as you are concerned, the service is free. Now many argue that the price of the commission is already built into the price, but since you are going to be paying the same price whether you book your plans or your agent does, you might as well use the agent.

Save money: A good travel agent will have a computer that can access virtually all of the prices being offered by the major players in the travel industry. By using a travel agent you are more likely to obtain the best price available for your travel plans.

NOTE: Some travel agents are offered special bonuses by some companies to steer business their way. Ask the agent to show you the prices of all competitors for your specific travel needs to make sure your pocketbook is being cared for and not the agent's.

Convenience. Twenty minutes of your time discussing your plans with your travel agent can save you hours of arranging things yourself. Your agent can find out all of the information you need to plan the perfect vacation while you attend to the important things like buying new clothes to wear on that second honeymoon cruise.

Safety. There are a lot of fraudulent travel schemes waiting to snare the unwary. Your travel agent will be able to research any company that is offering a good price to check on their authenticity. For example, one type of travel scam is the offering of a low plane fare to some exotic locale by a charter airline. Many a traveler has paid for such tickets only to find that their plane to paradise does not exist. Your travel agent can take steps to ensure that the price offered is valid and that the company seeking your business is a legitimate enterprise.

Information. The business of travel agents is travel. They should be up-to-date on what you need to know about the place you are going. They should also know about what's new and different under the sun in case you want some good ideas about where to go.

Obtain Necessary Paperwork In Advance Of Travel: If you are planning to travel overseas, there may be some paperwork before your trip. For example, you may need a passport. It can take weeks to obtain it if you don't have one, so plan ahead and get yours early. You should also find out if you need a visa (permission to enter the country) from the country you are traveling to. If so, you need to find the country's nearest consulate and go through their red tape in order to get your visa.

Find Out What To Do If Something Goes Wrong: There are probably few feelings in the world worse than being in a strange place where you don't know anyone and something goes wrong. Ask your travel agent what to do if you have a medical problem, reservation snafu or other crisis which threatens to ruin your trip.

Ask If There Are Senior Discounts Available: One of the benefits of growing older is that you qualify for senior discounts for the purchase of many services and products. This is especially true when it comes to travel since the industry earns a large percentage of its profits from traveling seniors. If discounts are available, be sure you understand the fine print since there may be restrictions that apply. For example, airline discounts must usually be purchased in advance and are frequently nonrefundable.

If You Have Special Needs, Inform The Travel Agent In Advance: Many seniors have special dietary or other needs that obviously can't be left at home when they travel. If this applies to you, be sure to tell your travel agent to "spread the word." For example, if you are going on a cruise and need a salt-free diet, the cruise line must be told ahead of time to make sure that your special needs are met.

Use A Major Credit Card To Book Your Trip: It always makes sense to use a credit card to pay for your travel since many offer special travel amenities such as life insurance to those who do so. Ask your credit card company for details on any special travel benefits they may have available for you.

Take Sensible Precautions: Wherever you are going, it pays to be safe. Here are a few safety tips to help:

—Don't carry large amounts of cash; instead of money, use travelers checks. Also, don't take your expensive jewelry with you. It's too easy to lose or have stolen.

—Bring a medical summary of your health history including a list of the types and doses of medicines you take and anything you may be allergic to.

—Purchase travel insurance. Ask your travel agent for details.

—Bring an extra pair of glasses in case yours are lost or broken.

—Leave your itinerary with a friend or relative and check in every so often so that everyone knows that you are fine and are having fun.

—Find out if there are any special health precautions that must be taken before you leave.

SENIOR CENTERS

Do you want to dance? Would you like to play a weekly bingo game? Want to take trips to local sights of interest and vacations to faraway places? Would you like to get a nutritious and tasteful meal five days a week for a little more than a dollar a day? Would you like to attend lectures on the issues that are important to you? Would you like free blood pressure screenings? Would you like to join a band? Would you like an inexpensive manicure? Would you like to join an exercise class? Would you like to learn how to oil paint? Would you like to learn how to play the organ? Would you like to play in bridge tournaments? Would you like to learn how to hablar espanol? Would you like a place where you can find all sorts of information and help with a wide variety of senior problems and issues? Would you like to meet a lot of people just like you? Would you like to do all of this and more and all under one roof? Then get thee to your local senior center where good times and quality living await your beck and call.

Senior centers are a cornerstone of the Older Americans

Act. Their purpose is to help seniors enjoy life to the fullest and to otherwise assist them in leading active and meaningful lives. Of course, as you would expect from such a broad-based and action packed program, the requirements for entry are pretty stiff: You have to be age 60 or over and able to either care for yourself or bring someone with you who can take care of you. That's it.

I have visited these hubs of senior life and have found them to be very "up" and exciting places where seniors truly appear to be having a heck of a good time. But I'll let the seniors tell you themselves.

George: Age 79—"There's everything here. I don't know of anything more that people could look for. There is just everything here. I met Adeline here. We're what you call 'an item.'"

Adeline: Age 78—"I love the dancing, and the ease with which widowers and widows can get together for socializing."

Phil: Age 73—"There's a very warm approach here. Someone's always getting a friendly hug or a kiss on the cheek. For some, it's the only love they receive."

May: Age 69—"This is family away from family. Many of us have families that live far away and can only see us on special occassions. Here, I have family everyday. It's most rewarding."

Peg: Age 71—"The people at the senior center try to solve the problems of the seniors whether it's legal, physical, financial or whatever. If the staff can't help us, they can refer us to those who can. There's so much information available here. It makes life a lot less frustrating."

George: (nutritional director)—"One of the most important things we do at the center is to make sure that everyone gets at least one good square meal a day. I serve anywhere from 60 people a day to roughly 300. And let me tell you, it's a labor of love."

I guess that about says it all.

6

Planning
For The
Final Curtain

Putting Your Affairs In Order

The Probate System; Wills; Estate Planning; Living
Trusts; Testamentary Trusts; Joint Tenancy; Gift
Giving; Living Wills; Conservatorships; Powers Of
Attorney; Preplanned Funeral Services

We may go years, even decades and only experience death
intellectually. We know we are going to die someday—we just
don't believe it. I mean, what kind of a world would it be
without us in it, right?

Then, something happens. Perhaps, as occurred with me,
a parent dies. Or, maybe we become seriously ill and are
introduced to Old Man Death who smiles, waves and says he'll
be seeing us sometime. But whatever the cause, we suddenly
know that old truth deep within our bones; no one gets out of
here alive, except perhaps George Burns. If we can't change
the inevitable we can at least prepare for it. At best, this may
mean that when we go, we go on our terms with dignity and in
control of our own destiny. Even if that is not possible, we can
make sure that those we leave behind are benefitted most and
inconvenienced least by our passing. And that truly is a gift of
great love.

WILLS AND ESTATE PLANNING

As long as there have been governments, there have been intricate schemes to tax the governed. And as long as there have been the governed, there have been equally intricate counter-schemes to avoid the taxes. After all, where there's a will and a lawyer, there's usually a way. Back and forth they go; a tax is levied, parried with a loophole and then that loophole is filled with a new tax that somehow creates a new loophole.

Out of this grand tradition come estate taxes and probate fees, estate planning lawyers and financial planners. This all makes planning one's affairs a very complicated affair itself.

THE PROBATE SYSTEM:

At this point, a general overview of the rules of the game are in order. As we all know, during life we accumulate money, property and other material possessions that are called an "estate." Alas, we also know you can't take it with you. When you go, you go. Your estate stays. Just ask King Tut. His estate ended up in a museum.

When the time comes, your estate will probably be "probated." A probate is a legal action that takes place in Probate Court. The purpose of a probate is to distribute your property among the living, (either to the persons directed by you in a legal document called a will, or by operation of law to your nearest relatives). However, there's a catch and that is: before distribution, your estate will be valued, your just debts paid, taxes (if any) levied and fees subtracted from the estate to pay for lawyers and executors who do all of this work.

These fees and taxes can take a major hunk out of the estate. That's why most people wish to have their estate distributed as they have specified in their will but avoid estate taxes as much as possible. Here's a general overview of the different ways that they go about it.

WILLS:

There are varieties from the simple to the complicated. The purpose of a will is to direct the court to dispose of your property and personal possessions according to your stated desires. A will can also name the person or persons you want to act as guardian of your minor children should you die before they become adults. Moreover, the provisions of a will can be used to reduce probate expenses to your estate. A will can also be used to disinherit anyone who would otherwise be entitled to a share of your property.

Each state has its own laws regarding the validity of wills and probate. However, the following general principals need to be discussed:

A Handwritten Will Can Be Valid In Some States: Many people try to avoid the cost of a lawyer by writing their wills out by hand. This is called a holographic will and some states do honor them provided they are entirely handwritten, dated and signed by the person making the will. They are not valid in many states, so be sure to ask a local lawyer about the laws where you live. The document must, within its terms, have clearly been intended to be a will, or it may be ruled invalid by the court. A holographic will does not have to be witnessed, but it always helps.

Some of the drawbacks of a handwritten will are:

—You may fail to use the proper language and part or all that you tried to accomplish with your will can be invalidated.

—Improper legal language that a lawyer would have avoided may also create additional problems for your estate. This almost always translates into additional money charged to your estate when probated.

—If you scratch out a word and then don't rewrite the whole will, a court may rule that your will is invalid.

—Disappointed heirs are more likely to challenge handwritten wills than wills prepared by lawyers because those tend to be more airtight.

—A holographic will may not be valid where you live or where you move to after it has been written.

Unless you have a very small estate or find yourself about to be in a life or death situation, I strongly suggest you don't practice law on yourself.

Some States Allow Fill In The Blank Wills: As consumers have tried to break the monopoly lawyers have over the practice of law, a new type of will has been created in some states called the "statutory will." A statutory will is a fill in the blank form which is specifically permitted by state law. Those with smaller estates can take advantage of this type of will with little fear that it will be invalidated. However, if you seek to alter the form in any way, all bets may be off.

Formal Wills Can Range From The Simple To The Complex: For our purposes, a formal will shall be defined as one that is prepared by a lawyer, typed, dated, signed and witnessed as required by the laws of the state in which you reside. Formal wills can be simple, such as stating that you leave the entire estate to your spouse; and if he or she predeceases you, to your children. Or they can be very complex with many built-in contingencies and/or the creation of multiple trusts which can last for decades. The cost of a simple will is rather modest, usually in the low hundreds for a husband and wife, while a very complicated document can cost many thousands of dollars to prepare.

A Will Allows You To Name The Person You Trust The Most To Manage Your Estate During Probate: When a decedent's estate is probated, someone has to be appointed by the court to manage the estate, pay the outstanding bills and formally take the action necessary to carry out the will's marching orders. This person or financial institution is called the "executor" if named in the will, and an "administrator" if appointed by the court when there is no will. This is a position of very grave responsibility as evidenced by the fact that many an estate has been dissipated by poor management. A will allows you to name the person or financial institution you believe is best for the job, thereby reducing the chance of a costly snafu.

Only One Will Is Valid At A Time: You can draft as many wills in a lifetime as you wish, but only the latest in time is ever valid (assuming that it has been properly prepared and witnessed). The very act of writing a new valid will voids all previously drafted wills.

Wills Can Be Revoked At Anytime: Assuming you are of sound mind and that no legal impediments exist that could prevent you from revoking (invalidating) your will such as mental incompetence, you may revoke your will at any time by destroying or defacing it or by simply writing a new one.

A Properly Prepared Will Is Very Difficult To Challenge: If you believe that the provisions of your will are likely to create hard feelings and the possibility of a lawsuit to invalidate its terms (such as if you intend to disinherit a child or other close relative), be sure that a lawyer prepares your will. He or she should be able to draft a will that is airtight according to the laws of your state. Wills stand or fall on their use of language. A poorly drafted will may have lots of loopholes, thereby increasing the likelihood of a challenge in court.

NOTE: Getting married after a will has been written may affect its legality. If you marry, either add a codicil or write a new will that takes into account your new legal

> status. Conversely, a divorce may not affect the will at all. So, if you no longer want the former apple of your eye to receive a piece of the pie, you had better talk to a lawyer.

Wills Can Be Modified: You can write a new will at any time. However, if the changes you wish to make are relatively minor in nature, you may not have to go to the expense of drafting an entire new document. Instead, you can add a codicil that makes the changes you want while allowing the rest of the will to remain undisturbed. The laws regarding codicils also vary from state to state, so if you have any questions about the procedure, ask a lawyer who practices probate law in your locality.

ESTATE PLANNING:

One of the problems with wills is that in order to be enforced, they must usually be probated and this can be very expensive. Thus, one of the things that many people want to do while planning for their demise is to fix things so that their loved ones can avoid the expenses of probate and/or federal and state estate or death taxes altogether. This can be easier said than done.

A whole industry exists to service this great desire to avoid the expenses of probate. The generic term for process is "estate planning." The following are some of the principle weapons in the estate planner's arsenal:

The Living Trust: The "Big Bertha" of estate planning is undoubtedly the living trust that does away with probate altogether, and saves the estate thousands of dollars in attorneys fees and probate costs. Living trusts, however, can be so complicated that many lawyers don't understand how they work.

In very simplified terms, the living trust works something like this: the "trustor," that's you, transfers all of his or her property into a legal entity known as a trust. The property of the trust is controlled by a person known as a "trustee," again you. At this point, legally, you no longer own the property (the trust does) but you do control it as long as you have made yourself trustee. So nothing really changes unless you make someone else the trustee, in which case that person controls the property.

The trust is established to benefit specifically named persons called "beneficiaries." Now, here's the fun part; you can be the beneficiary and name others, called "alternate beneficiaries," to take your place should you die. This means that during your lifetime, all of the benefits of your property will go to you as they always did. It also means that you can name as alternate beneficiaries to the trust those persons you would have named to receive your property in your will.

The effect of all of this is to pass all of your property directly to the alternate beneficiaries free of probate when you die. The reason you can do this is that technically you did not own any property and thus there is nothing to be probated upon your death. Clever, no?

Now, I must emphasize that living trusts are not perfect. They do not avoid estate taxes and creditors can go after trust property to force the payment of debts long after your death unlike a probate which has a relatively short time limit for creditors to come forward. They are also expensive to have a lawyer prepare, especially when compared to a will. But for many, the living trust is the ideal way to preserve their estate while maintaining total control over their property during their lifetime.

NOTE: A lawyer can prepare many variations of the living trust, so be sure to discuss all the possibilities with one who is an expert in the field of living trusts. Be sure you understand the document thoroughly before you sign it.

Be sure the lawyer prepares a will to go with the trust to take care of property not formally made a part of the trust and to accomplish the other things that a will can do, such as name guardians for minor children.

The Testamentary Trust: A testamentary trust is a trust that is created in your will and takes effect upon your death. The principal purpose of a testamentary trust is to avoid estate taxes and to control the way your money is spent once you're gone.

Married couples who wish to reduce federal estate taxes typically choose the testamentary trust to accomplish this task because the federal government does not tax property left to surviving spouses, although they do tax all other property exceeding $600,000. The couple can leave all of their property in trust to their children or grandchildren and have the income from the property used to support the surviving spouse. This can save a lot in taxes since the children technically receive the property in trust upon the death of the first spouse, not through probate upon the other's death. While the estate is taxed fully under the law when the first spouse dies, there is a substantial reduction in taxes when the second spouse dies.

In addition, the surviving spouse can be protected since the trust can be drafted so as to allow him or her to use the income and even invade the principal during his or her lifetime, depending upon the terms of the trust. Thus, taxes can be saved with little or no inconvenience to the surviving spouse.

A second use of a testamentary trust is to protect people from themselves. For example, if the maker of the trust or the "testator" dies fearing that his spoiled son will squander the inheritance, then he can ensure that sonny boy only receives a limited amount per year so as to preserve the estate for the boy's lifetime.

I must emphasize that this is only a cursory discussion of the subject; lawyers spend years learning the ins and outs of trusts. There are many other examples of appropriate testamentary trusts than the one given here, so do ask a lawyer for more information. In addition, I must warn you that unlike living trusts, probate is not avoided by testamentary trusts. On the other hand, living trusts don't avoid estate taxes. However, if you have a large estate and a good reason to use the testamentary trust, it can be a potent weapon in your personal crusade against higher taxes.

Joint Tenancy: Many people try to avoid probate by placing their property, most often real estate, in joint tenancy. This can avoid probate because when one joint tenant dies, his or her surviving joint tenant automatically becomes the owner of the other's interest in the property. This is known in legal circles as "the right of survivorship." Probate is avoided over the piece of property that was held in joint tenancy since at the moment of death the deceased legally ceased to have an ownership interest in the property.

Nonetheless, placing property in joint tenancy is not really a good idea, although it does avoid probate on that piece of property. Here are the drawbacks:

—You cease to enjoy exclusive control over the property. Once someone else's name is added to property as a joint tenant, he or she becomes an equal owner. This means that you would have to get the joint tenant's permission to sell the property. If it were refused, you'd have to sue to force a sale, and then you might only receive your proportionate share of the funds, less all of the attorneys' fees and costs involved.

—Conversely, once someone else becomes a co-owner, he or she could force you to sell.

—If the joint tenant is in debt, his or her share of the property may be subject to attachment by creditors.

—Chances are that estate taxes will not be avoided.

If you are still interested in using joint tenancy to avoid probate, ask a lawyer to fashion a contract with the proposed joint tenant which might avoid some of these pitfalls.

Gift Giving: One very effective way of reducing the cost of probate and estate taxes is to give the property away to those whom you would have left it to in your will before you die. The reason that probate and taxes will be lower is that the value of your estate will be lower since you gave part of it away.

If this appeals to you, there are some things you should be aware of:

—If you give more than $10,000 per year in cash or property to any individual or non-charitable institution or entity, you will be subject to a federal gift tax. (A married couple can give $20,000 before being subject to taxes.) Thus, if you have a great deal to give away, you'd better start sooner than later or spread the wealth around if you wish to avoid taxes.

—Certain gifts given within three years of death may still be subject to estate taxes. The most common example of this is the ownership of a life insurance policy.

—Gift giving can come in many forms other than the obvious present wrapped in foil. For example, forgiving a just debt is a gift, so is an irrevocable trust (one that cannot be taken back). Permitting someone to withdraw money you deposited from a joint bank account is also considered a gift.

—Once a gift has been legally "given," it cannot be taken back. A gift is given if a mentally competent person voluntarily delivers the gift to the person receiving it. Once the person receiving the gift accepts it, the transaction is complete. At that point, you cannot change your mind and legally force a return of the given object.

—If you give a gift to a minor, things can become complicated. This is because most states require that property held by minors be supervised by an adult. This usually involves the appointment of a custodian, such as a relative or financial institution, who will administer the property on behalf of the minor until he or she reaches majority. Be sure to consult a lawyer before giving any gift of substance to a minor.

Of course, there are reasons other than pecuniary for giving gifts. There is the intangible such as seeing the delight on your loved one's face when he or she receives that special something. In my book (which this is), it's better to see the joy a gift gives "in the flesh" rather than "in spirit."

> **NOTE:** If you are going to give a substantial gift or one involving real property, first consult with a lawyer. Each state has different laws regarding gift taxes. In addition, gift giving can become very complicated transactions. Besides, there may be ways to accomplish your estate planning goals without giving up control over valued property.

This ends our discussion of wills and estate planning. My purpose has been to introduce you to the field, not give comprehensive information or legal advise. A lawyer can do that only after he or she has has an opportunity to study the facts of your case. If you want further information, consult with a qualified attorney.

PREPARING FOR THE WORST

At one time or another, many older people suffer temporary or permanent disabilities which may prevent them from making decisions about their own lives. If caught unprepared, such an emergency can have implications far beyond the immediate questions of health and welfare. A vacuum will be created where no one is in charge of the incapacitated person's affairs. This can lead to a mad scramble to "put things in order" and can cause family discord. In extreme circumstances, families have even been known to litigate themselves apart over "what to do about Mom."

A little foresight can prevent the tragedy of a serious

illness or injury from being compounded by family infighting. In addition, by hoping for the best and preparing for the worst, each of us can remain in significant control of our own destinies even if we are completely unconscious.

DECISIONS OVER LIFE AND DEATH:

While most of us fear death, it almost pales in comparison to the loathing most of us feel about being kept alive by extraordinary means after the brain has ceased to function. How can you make sure that this "living in limbo" does not happen? After all, can we really expect those who love us to be able to summon up the courage to order the doctor to "pull the plug"? And if they do, are we damning them to a lifetime of guilt wondering whether they made the right decision?

Fortunately, you usually do have the power to take the decision out of the hands of others and keep it right where it belongs—with you.

Informed Consent: Every patient who is legally competent to make a decision has the absolute right to decide what kind of medical care he or she will receive or not receive. Under the law, this is known as the patient's right to informed consent. Simply stated, informed consent means that each patient has the right to know the pros and cons of each test and plan of treatment and the consequences of not proceeding and then has the right to make the choice of what will be done. If someone is told that they have a terminal illness, they can decide to fight it until "the clock runs out" or they can decide to allow nature to take its course. No one can force you to do anything you don't want to.

Living Wills: But what happens to patients who are incapable of making an informed consent or refusal? Well, if they showed a little foresight before they were physically or mentally incapacitated, they can still speak for themselves through legal documents generically called living wills (the name of the document in your state may vary).

By signing a living will while you are competent, you decide whether or not doctors should take extraordinary artificial means to preserve your life if you suffer from an incurable injury or disease. Many states also allow their citizens to sign a power of attorney (the name of the document may vary) which delegates the power to make this decision to a trusted friend or loved one in the event the patient is unable to give informed consent.

If you are interested in a living will, ask your attorney or local medical society to provide one for you. Read the instructions carefully before filling it out or, better yet, have your attorney fill it in for you. He or she won't charge much for the service, and you'll sleep better knowing that your living will has been properly prepared.

> **NOTE:** Living wills are not legally binding in every state. However, even if they have no legal effect, filling one out will, at the very least, inform your family and your doctors about how you wish to be treated which will make their decision that much easier.

MAINTAINING YOUR ESTATE:

Of course, every decision that must be made in the event of incapacitation does not concern issues of life and death. More commonly, a plan of action will be needed to manage the incapacitated person's estate, at least until there is a return to competence if that event is likely to occur.

Conservatorships: Conservatorships allow a relative, friend or other qualified person to be appointed by the Probate Court to manage the financial affairs of someone who is unable to do so themselves under the supervision of the court. They can be obtained over the "person" of an incompetent person and can be entered into voluntarily or involuntarily under certain conditions. Ask a lawyer who practices in the field of probate law to find out what the laws are in your state.

Powers of Attorney: A power of attorney is a legal document that grants someone else, called an "attorney in fact," the authority to act on your behalf. The authority granted by the "principal" or the person who signs the power of attorney can be broad or limited both in terms of what can be managed and the time during which the power is in effect.

There are two different types of powers of attorney:

The Power Of Attorney. A "simple" power of attorney allows you to delegate the power to manage part or all of your affairs . For example, if you are going on a world cruise, you may wish to appoint someone to pay your bills, manage your assets and otherwise keep your affairs in order. Or if you are selling some property and want an expert to handle the transaction for you, a power of attorney would permit that person to handle the sale in all of its aspects.

As principal, you have the right to set the limits on your attorney in fact's powers. You may wish to grant the attorney in fact the power to virtually control your financial life. Or you may wish to "reserve" powers for yourself, such as the right to collect income from rental property you own. In other words, the scope of the attorney in fact's powers go only as far as you define in the power of attorney document. Likewise, you can limit the time during which the attorney in fact has the power to act on your behalf. The power of attorney automatically ceases upon the incapacity or death of the principal. In addition, it can be revoked by the principal at any time.

The Durable Power Of Attorney. The word "durable" in front of "power of attorney" creates a distinction that makes a big difference. Whereas a power of attorney ceases upon the incapacity of the principal, the whole point of a durable power of attorney is to put in place an attorney who can act on the principal's behalf during incapacitation, thus avoiding a court ordered conservatorship.

Durable powers of attorney come in two styles to fit the taste of the most discriminating principal. The "regular" durable power of attorney goes into effect as soon as it has been validly entered by the principal or on the date set forth in the document itself. The "springing" power of attorney does not go into effect unless the principal becomes incapacitated, at which time it immediately "springs" into effect. The durable power of attorney can grant to the attorney in fact the power to make decisions regarding the principal's health such as whether to consent to treatment or hire or fire medical professionals. It can even permit the attorney in fact to decide whether the principal should be kept alive by artificial means.

Durable powers of attorney can be revoked at any time by the principal so long as he or she is competent. Like the power of attorney, "durables" cease upon the death of their maker.

Before you sign a power of attorney or become an attorney in fact for someone else, I strongly urge you to discuss the matter with an attorney for the following reasons:

—As with most legal documents, the formalities and the wording used in a power of attorney are very important. The lawyer can help make sure the document is validly prepared and executed and can make sure that you delegate only those powers you wish.

—Unlike a conservatorship, there is no formal review by a court or anyone else over the acts of an attorney in fact. This means that the potential harm to your estate (or even your person) caused by the intentional misconduct or negligent acts of the attorney in fact can be enormous.

—An attorney in fact is a "fiduciary" to the principal. This means that the attorney in fact cannot simply treat the principal as he or she would anyone else. A fiduciary is under a legal duty to act in the highest good faith and must avoid even the appearance of conflict of interest. In addition, the fiduciary must not commingle the assets of the principal with his or her own funds. Failure to strictly adhere to the highest fiduciary ethics by an attorney in fact can lead to a costly lawsuit.

—A living trust can do all that a durable power of attorney can do if you nominate someone else as trustee or alternate trustee. (The trustee controls the property place in trust.) While the living trust avoids probate, it also costs much more to prepare than a power of attorney since it is a far more complicated document.

PRE-PLANNING THE LAST GOOD-BYE

Since this chapter is basically about preparing for worst case scenarios, why don't we talk about cemetaries and tombstones. And while we're at it, let's talk about a true gift of love that you can give to your family after you're gone. Let's talk about pre-planning your last good-bye.

Why do I say that such a morbid subject can be the subject of great love? I speak from experience. My grandmother was really special. She immigrated here from Italy when only 16 and worked her family over to America before she was 20. She was widowed at an early age and raised two children at a time when there was no social security or other government help. She supported her family by washing and styling women's hair year after year until her nose was lightly shaded a permanent blue from all of the dye she had to handle. She worked until both children married and started families of their own. Even then, Grandma worked. And with the money she earned, she travelled to Italy, Tahiti, Mexico and the Carribean.

In 1978, Grandma died at the age of 86. And when my father, my uncle and I went to the funeral home, we found that everything had been planned in advance. Grandma did not want us to sit through complete descriptions of funeral services and coffins. Ever sensible, she had alrealy purchased her plot, all we had to do was sign and pay with the money she had set aside for her final good-bye. I can't tell you how much easier her thoughtfulness made a difficult time for us all.

Most of us choose not to think about all that must go into the last good-bye. But imagine having to make all of the decisions that go into a funeral and burial while in the depth of shock and grief that the passing of a parent or other beloved relative will bring.

Here are the realities of what must be dealt with when that time arrives:

Mortuary Services: Mortuary services include picking the remains up from the place of death, embalming (or holding the body in cold storage until the funeral), securing signatures and death certificates, body preparation if there is to be a viewing and the use of the facilities.

Mortuaries differ in price, size and sometimes even in "specialty" such as catering to certain religious or cultural groups. This diversity, which can be very broad, means that the family is likely to obtain the best service at the best price if, to put it frankly, they "shop around."

Now can you imagine "shopping around" when your favorite uncle has just passed away? Of course you can't. And most families don't. That's why you can do them all a big favor when your time comes and shop around for them beforehand. You can arrange everything yourself so that all the family has to do is call. The funeral home will do what has to be done, as specified by you, while your family attends to its own needs.

Final Resting Place: The next ordeal a family must face when there has been a death is choosing whether to cremate the remains or have the body buried. This is something you can specify in your will. Even if you do, your family still has to tour the local cemetary to choose the right spot. Cemetary space is a lot like housing, the better the view and the "neighborhood," the higher the cost of the land. You can spare your loved ones that awful experience by buying ahead of time. Such forethought also guarantees the space you want at the price you believe you can afford.

> **NOTE:** Once sold, the cemetary will not buy the land back. So, before you buy a plot, be sure it is where you wish to be buried.

Funeral Arrangements: There's a lot more to planning a funeral than you might think. For example, picking the casket can be very traumatic. Imagine being filled with grief and touring a showroom of caskets that would put some Cadillacs to shame? It's tough. Now imagine that money is a consideration, and the low priced model just doesn't look good enough? Money you would rather have your children spend on themselves may very well end up being spent on you. Pre-select, and that can be avoided. The same goes for the plaque. Plaques can be very expensive, depending on size and the amount of wording. By making arrangements ahead of time you can make your wishes known, taking a great burden off of the shoulders of those you love.

There's much more to discuss about funerals and burials, but I think the point has been made. If you have any questions about pre-planning, contact your local mortuaries and cemetaries for further information.

> **NOTE:** There is a difference between "preplanning" and "prepaying" for funerals. And, be warned, there are some scam artists operating out there in the prepaid funeral business. If you are thinking of prepaying, be sure to investigate the funeral home thoroughly before you sign a contract. Have your lawyer review it just to be safe. Also, be sure that any money you pay goes into a trust account until time of need rather than the operators' pocket.

You can also pre-arrange cremation services with a cremation society. Upon death, the cremation society will pick up the body, deal with the formalities such as death certificates, perform the cremation and return them in a proper container to the family or "scatter" them as permitted by state law. And all of this for thousands of dollars less than traditional mortician services and burial.

Many financial institutions will allow you to establish an account which is specifically earmarked to pay for funeral expenses. Ask your local bank or savings and loan for more details.

There are a few other things that need to be mentioned about funerals and funeral homes:

1)The Federal Trade Commission publishes a free funeral rule guide. You can obtain it by writing to:

The Federal Trade Commission
Sixth and Pennsylvania Avenues, NW
Washington D.C. 20036

2)There is a consumer arbitration program available through the National Funeral Directors Association should tragedy in your life be made worse by a funeral home's improper conduct. The program has many benefits to consumers.

—Binding arbitration is available allowing a quick and inexpensive resolution of the dispute.

—The program is available to anyone who has complaints about a funeral home's services during the previous twelve months. That means you can get over the worst of your grief before filing and not forfeit your rights.

—The arbitration relies solely on written testimony, thus valuable time need not be taken from work to attend any hearings.

—The arbitration is free, thus the fear of throwing good

money after bad should not keep you from seeking redress of grievances.

—If you win and the funeral director refuses or can't pay you the money that is owed, there is a Consumer Security Fund that will pay you the restitution you are owed.

For more information on the program contact:

The Funeral Service
Arbitration Program
P.O. Box 27641
Milwaukee, WI. 53227

7

Into Each Life
A Little Rain
Must Fall

Coping With Senior Problems

Senior Abuse; The Terminal Illness Of A Spouse; Hospice Care; Grief Counseling; Widowhood; Debilitation; Adult Day Care; Meals On Wheels; Telephone Reassurance; Emergency Response Systems; Utility And Tax Assistance Programs

Everybody has problems and we're all looking for solutions, but not just any solution; we want the perfect solution that will make everything better again.

There's an old and very wise joke that illustrates this point. The joke goes something like this:

A grandmother and her young grandson are walking along the beach enjoying each other's company and the breeze by the shore. Suddenly, a huge tidal wave strikes which sweeps the young boy out to sea. Distraught, the grandmother looks to the sky and prays, "Please God, send my grandson back to me. I've been good my whole life, and I never asked for anything. Now, I'm asking. Please."

Suddenly, another huge wave crashes on the shore, and to the woman's delight, her beloved grandson lands unhurt at her feet. The woman picks the boy up, looks him over from top to bottom and, looking to the sky, speaks again, "Thank you Lord, but he was wearing a hat!"

Behind every problem, there is usually a solution. It may not be perfect, but it is a rare situation that can't be helped with a creative response. This chapter is all about finding solutions for problems that typically afflict seniors.

SENIOR ABUSE

We have a silent crisis in our midst. It is found in large cities and small towns. It strikes the rich as well as the middle class and the poor. No one likes to talk about it, but it must be addressed. That problem is senior abuse.

Senior abuse occurs when an elderly person is not being cared for with the respect and dignity that is the right of every human being. Neglect can be just as harmful to a senior citizen as physical abuse and is usually more common. There are many signs that indicate neglect, including weight loss, uncleanliness and the inability to function mentally when there is no indication of physical impairment. In an institution, bedsores are a good indication that the senior is not being moved. Sheets and nightgowns that are continually soiled by waste are strong evidence that basic hygiene is being ignored. Whether private or institutional, any kind of neglect is a serious problem that should not be ignored.

While child abuse receives a great deal of media attention in this country, there is also an alarming increase in elder abuse that receives far less attention. The abuse often comes at the hands of the older person's own children or close relatives. It can also occur in nursing homes or other residential facilities. Just as with children, the older victim may be reluctant to talk about the problem out of guilt or fear of retaliation. Signs that abuse is taking place are often obvious, such as unexplained bruises and cuts. Other signs of abuse can be more subtle, ranging from fear of the caregiver to abnormal drowsiness due to excessive sedation.

It is sometimes very difficult to detect abuse or neglect

unless someone actually witnesses the wrongful acts. Many signs of abuse may be completely innocent. For example, many older people do fall more frequently than they did when they were younger and the falls tend to be more serious.

What should you do if you or an older friend has been abused or neglected? If you witness or even suspect abuse or neglect, contact your local police and they will direct you to the proper authorities.

When talking to the agency investigator or social worker, try to be as detailed as you can about why you believe a problem exists. Saying something doesn't seem right isn't enough to justify utilizing the strained resources of the agency. Try to be more detailed in your description, stating, for example, something like this: "For the last two months I have seen bruises all over the man's arms and face, and yesterday he had a fat lip. When I asked him what was wrong, he refused to look me in the eye and mumbled something about falling. When I told him I was going to ask the administrator what was going on, he begged me not to, stating that he would get in trouble." A detailed description gives the agency worker enough evidence to investigate.

Once the agency believes there is reasonable evidence a problem exists, the state or local agency in charge of stopping abuse and neglect cases will conduct an investigation. If they believe that there is misconduct, they will step in to remedy the situation. Agency intervention can range from counseling for distressed families to finding immediate housing for the abused person. Medical assistance is also available, and in severe cases, referrals can be made to the judicial authorities for criminal prosecution or license revocations.

NOTE: If you suffer from abuse, you must cooperate with the authorities. Failure to do so cripples their ability to protect you and may increase the likelihood that the abuse will continue.

> **NOTE:** The quality, commitment and funding of these social welfare agencies vary from city to city as does the strength of the safety net they provide. For more information on the procedures and effectiveness of the protective services in your area, contact your local protective services agency, a nearby chapter of the AARP or other senior advocacy group or the office of your local government representative.

THE TERMINAL ILLNESS OF A SPOUSE

When we marry, we usually make a vow in which we promise to love and cherish our spouse "in good times and bad times, in sickness and in health, 'til death do us part." Unfortunately, one spouse usually dies before the other and must face the difficult task of seeing their beloved through the trials and travails of a terminal illness.

In earlier times, the family and community could be counted on to support a terminally ill patient. Meals would be prepared; aunts, cousins and neighbors would drop in to lend a hand with the chores and the shopping. A strong bond would be created to help the dying person and the spouse cope with the circumstances.

But times have changed. Many families are not close, and even those who are may be spread across the country. Because we have become a very mobile society, community ties are not as strong as they once were. Where once a whole family and community could have been relied upon to help, there may now be a vacuum.

In recent years this vacuum has been recognized and met by a variety of services. Among them are the following:

Hospice Care: A hospice isn't just a place, it's a philosophy that combines loving care and support with medical science's ability to reduce the pain and suffering of terminal illnesses. If a patient decides to fight to the end, hospice care is not the ticket. However, if the decision is to let nature take its course, then hospice may be an appropriate option.

When a patient agrees to hospice care, he or she gives informed consent to discontinue any extraordinary life-saving medical care. In addition, the patient agrees that when the time comes, no effort will be made to resuscitate him or her or to artificially prolong life. Instead, the hospice team will work very hard to control pain and provide loving support. The idea then is not to save a life but to help make it as comfortable and dignified as possible.

Hospice usually begins once a physician has diagnosed a patient as having a terminal condition. Once a hospice provider is selected, the patient and the family become the focus of the professional services which are available. Most of the care is given in the home. This means that there must be family or friends willing to undertake the responsibility of being the dying person's primary caregiver. Many hospice providers also have hospital space available for those times when the family needs a break or when the patient will be better served in a hospital setting. These hospital rooms are usually more "homey" than most and will have a lounge and bed space available for families who wish to stay close.

The hospice team is made up of the patient's primary care physician, nurses who visit the home regularly and psychologists or social workers who work with the patient and family in order to help them adjust to the unfortunate circumstances. Homemakers are also provided under appropriate circumstances and clergy are made available for those who desire such support. Also assigned to the case is a specially trained volunteer "friend" whose only job is to be there, to talk, to sympathize and otherwise help all involved work through the death experience. However, the most important team member may just be the family members who are taught the skills needed to give true quality care to the dying loved one.

Hospice care does not stop when the "end" comes. Grieving family members continue to receive help and guidance in moving on with their lives. This grief counseling can be one of the most beneficial services that the hospice provides.

When selecting a hospice, look for some of the following:

Is it Medicare Certified? If not, Medicare will not pay hospice benefits, but creative use of the home health care benefits under Medicare may be able to fill in the gap. Also, many hospices are nonprofit and many will not charge for their services if the patient or family cannot pay.

Is the hospice licensed by the state? Not all states require hospice providers to be licensed. If yours does, make sure the hospice is licensed.

Is the hospice a member of the National Hospice Organization? Since hospice care is a relatively new approach, there is still a wide variety of services offered by hospice providers. The National Hospice Organization has established minimum service standards for their members.

Do those you trust recommend the hospice provider? Many professionals work with the dying and their families all of the time. When selecting a hospice program, be sure to talk with your doctor, pastor, rabbi or priest and others such as social workers and nurses about the various programs which may be available. They should have a pretty good idea about the quality of programs which are available.

For more information on hospices contact:

National Hospice Organization
1901 N. Fort Myer Dr.
Arlington, Virginia 22209
(703) 243-5900

Grief Counseling: When a loved one has finally passed away, it is very important that the survivors recognize that they now need help. After all, it's tough to be left behind, especially after having a marriage that may have lasted for decades or a close relationship with a parent or sibling.

When someone is dying or has died, we experience the emotion called grief. Grief is usually expressed by crying, feelings of exhaustion and emptiness, a tightening of the throat, a sensation of choking and other physical pain. Loss of appetite is also common. There may also be a preoccupation with the dearly departed and memories of happy times, irritability with others and anger at the deceased for dying. This can cause guilt and further grief in a classic "Catch-22" situation.

Grief usually lasts from one to two years before it declines, allowing the resumption of normal life. Of course, that doesn't mean that feelings of loss disappear. My father has been gone for over five years and I still get choked up thinking about him. Of course, some will grieve longer and some shorter. We are all unique and so is our expression of grief.

Modern medicine and psychology has recognized that many have difficulties expressing their grief and have responded with a service called "grief counseling." Grief counseling may come in the form of a support group made up of cancer patients and their families. It may be group therapy for the recently widowed, or it may be one-on-one sessions with a psychologist or therapist, or it may take place as a part of hospice care. Whatever its form, the purpose of grief counseling is to assist the survivors in experiencing their loss and then moving on to a new beginning.

Two of the most common things that a therapist may do are to give the grieving person permission to experience the emotion and then encourage him or her to express the feelings. While this may seem obvious, according to the experts, many people suppress grief and avoid the intense distress that goes with it. Part of this suppression may be cultural. Just compare funerals in America which are very proper and dignified affairs with funerals in other parts of the world which feature wailing, rending of clothes and gnashing of teeth. We tend to look down our noses at such open displays of grief, but I wonder which manner of mourning is the healthier?

A grieving patient and his or her counselor attempt to work through unresolved issues between the deceased and the survivor. The survivor may feel responsible for the death and may also have to overcome a fear of being alone.

Grief counseling is also there to assist those who do not express themselves in a "healthy" way. For example, some postpone their grief and act as if nothing has happened. This may not be healthy since the purpose of grief is to mourn the loss and then get on with things. Failure to mourn may debilitate. Some people get so depressed that they develop stress illnesses of their own.

Grief counseling programs exist in all parts of the nation. Many are run by hospitals. Others exist as part of hospice care. Many mental health professionals also place special emphasis in this field. If you are interested in more information, contact your local mental health association, your local chapter of the American Cancer Society or ask your physician for a referral.

WIDOWHOOD

In addition to grieving, a newly widowed person has many practical things to deal with. It may seem heartless to deal with these matters after being on the receiving end of such a loss but attending to these details does keep the widowed person busy and they serve as the first steps toward a new life.

The following is a short list of the tasks that face most widowed persons shortly after their spouse has passed away.

NOTE: Be sure to have a trusted friend or loved one assist with the details.

Funeral Arrangements: Arrangements must be made regarding the deceased's last rites and final resting place. Decisions such as whether to bury or cremate, to have a religious service or a large or small funeral, etc. must be made in a very brief period of time.

Collecting Papers: After a death, there are many documents that must be gathered together for processing.

—Part of the job of morticians and cremation societies is to obtain certified copies of the death certificate for the survivors. Be sure you get plenty of copies as the death certificate will be required many times in the days and weeks to come.

—Insurance policies must be collected and claims made.

—If the widowed person is applying for benefits, copies of the marriage certificate are required.

—If there is a will or living trust or other such document that takes effect upon the death of the deceased, it should be given to the lawyer's office.

—If military or veteran's benefits are claimed, the discharge papers should be collected. (If they are lost, write to the Department of Defense, National Personnel Record Center, 9700 Page Blvd. St. Louis, Mo. 63132.)

—The deceased's social security card or number is required in order to apply for death benefits.

—Deeds and other written evidence of holding title to property should be gathered in order to have the title changed for purposes of probate.

Processing The Work: There is so much to be done that it is usually a good idea to see a lawyer to receive some help, especially if there is a significant amount of property involved or else a probate will take place. There are others who can help ranging from trusted friends and relatives to organizations such as the AARP who have a Widowed Person's Service available to answer all of your questions.

Getting On With Life: Obviously, this may be easier said than done. But there comes a time when the paperwork has been processed, the legal formalities completed and grief is beginning to abate. This may be a good time to start a job or begin volunteer work. It may mean joining a social club or a senior center. Perhaps, it will involve selling the old homestead and moving nearer to the children. But whatever it means, it must be done.

For more information, contact:

> Widowed Persons Service
> AARP
> 1909 K St. N.W.
> Washington D.C. 20049
> (or contact your local chapter)

DEBILITATION

There's an old advertising line that said, "You're not getting older, you're getting better." I can't argue with that sentiment, but the plain truth of the matter is that the older we get, the more likely we are to have physical impairments that prevent us from living completely independent lives.

It used to be when physical debilitation occured, the immediate response of the family and medical world was, "get thee to a nursing home." No more. The Older Americans Act, Title XX of the Federal Social Security Act and other legislative and private initiatives have built a network of services which seeks to keep older people out of nursing homes, not in them.

I speak from experience. My paternal grandmother is 90 years old. She has had a tough life, losing four out of six children, a beloved husband and surviving a battle with cancer. She lives in a trailer park in Santa Barbara and loves it. The sea breezes keep her cool and her many friends visit and gossip over the park bingo game.

Unfortunately, my grandmother suffers from severe arthritis and has a tendency to get dizzy if she moves too fast. She falls easily, which makes it difficult for her to live alone much less get out and around. One of her daughters lives in

Sacramento, a son lives in Seattle and my mother and I live in Los Angeles, over 100 miles away.

This distance makes it very difficult to monitor my grandmother on a daily basis. One solution would be for her to move, but she refuses insisting that she is not going to lose her independence. Happily, in conjunction with her doctor, sufficient community services have been found to allow her to remain in control of her own destiny. She receives "Meals on Wheels," has a visiting nurse in on a regular basis and receives homemaking services. A volunteer does her shopping. She is also hooked up to an emergency response system and will soon have a wheelchair. She has some lovely neighbors who look in on her every day allowing her to live her life as she chooses.

My grandmother's story is not unique. Thanks to the depth and scope of service programs, millions of elderly Americans are able to maintain their lifestyles outside of a long-term care facility.

The following is a list and brief description of many of the services which are available. The availability of these programs may vary according to where you live, but most are easily obtainable.

Adult Day Care: Many seniors are able to live in the community because they have caregivers who "help them make it through the night." Often, these caregivers are children of other relatives who cannot always be physically present. Adult day care centers give the older person a place to go when the primary caregiver cannot be around.

Don't get the idea, however, that such day care centers are just warehouses where clients vegetate. Most provide hot meals, social services, speech therapy, medical and nursing care and recreation.

Most day care centers charge for their services (sometimes on a sliding scale), and most require that the patient be ambulatory, that is, not bedridden. Clients who need to use wheelchairs and/or walkers are most welcome.

Home Health Care: As described in Chapter 4, home health care providers offer a wide variety of services to their clients and patients. Among them are medical services such as the administration of medication, physical therapy, housekeeping and personal care (help with bathing and hygiene, etc.)

Home health care may be paid for by Medicare (within its limits), Medicaid, private insurance or by the patient and/or his or her family. Many providers are nonprofit organizations and may help even if funds are limited.

Meals On Wheels: This very valuable program delivers hot and nutritious meals right to the older person's home five days a week. Usually meals for weekends can be delivered frozen for later preparation. The cost is subsidized so that the recipient only pays $1.00-$1.50 for each meal.

Senior Companion Program: Senior Companions provide invaluable and free services ranging from helping with the shopping and writing letters to simply being a friend. I repeat, the services are free, regardless of the economic status of the recipient. So, if you or someone you love needs a friend who can be relied upon to be there, Senior Companion is the group to call.

Telephone Reassurance: Many community based organizations such as churches, synagogues and the AARP coordinate volunteer programs where a homebound elderly person is contacted by phone daily to make sure they are alright and to see if there are any needs that must be met.

Emergency Response Systems: Emergency response systems allow older citizens to reach help almost instantly in the event of an emergency. The programs vary, but usually involve the client wearing a necklace which has a button to push if help is ever needed. The button activates a unit that is connected to the telephone and automatically dials the emergency response center. From there, a neighbor or relative is contacted. The responder checks out the situation and coordinates with the emergency response center to see what must be done next.

The most famous provider of this type of service, and one with a fine reputation, is Lifeline. However, there are other companies coming on the market all of the time. Before you sign up for an emergency response system, I suggest you discuss the matter with your doctor or local hospital social worker to make sure you obtain the best and most reliable service in your area.

Utility And Tax Assistance Programs: One of the things that drives seniors from their homes and into long-term care facilities is the high cost of living. Many communities have responded to this by giving seniors a break on the cost of utilities and property taxes. Other programs also teach seniors how to use their utilities economically and to weatherize their homes. To see if such programs are available where you live, contact your Area Agency on Aging, your local chapter of the AARP or your local legislator or social welfare offices.

For further information on services available to seniors who need a helping hand, contact:

Administration on Aging
U.S. Department of Health and
Human Services
330 C St. S.W.
Washington D.C. 20201
(202) 245-0641

8

I've Been Had!

Avoiding Victimization In The Senior Years

Avoiding Quackery; Spotting Business Opportunity
Fraud; The Truth About Scams And Con Games;
Home Improvement Fraud; Preventing Crimes Of
Violence And Theft; Burglary Prevention

There should be a reward given to everyone who survives this destruction derby called life long enough to achieve seniordom. After all, longevity does not happen by accident. It takes moxie, fortitude, hard work and yes, a little bit of luck, to overcome the wars, diseases, accidents and general hard knocks of daily life.

Unfortunately, there is no such reward. And not only is there no reward, but far too many people reach seniordom only to find themselves beset by fears. At the top of the list is the fear of becoming the victim of a crime. There is an abundance of still more dangers.

Happily, it is not impossible to control fear. More importantly, it is possible for most to escape crime. All it takes is some guts, common sense, the willingness to be careful and not drawing the short straw.

QUACKERY

No, quackery is not a pond devoted to the raising of baby ducks. Rather, it is the promotion of a medical remedy that has not been proven to work. In legal terms, it is the crime of health fraud. The quack promises miracle cures and overnight results when such things do not exist. It is one of crime's most vile activities because it preys on people's fear. At best, quackery takes your money; at worst, it takes your life.

Senior citizens are the chief prey of quacks because they are the most vulnerable members of society. Vigilance is the key. The following are some of the more common cons perpetrated by the quack on the lookout for an easy mark and a quick buck:

Arthritis: Life can be difficult to those afflicted with arthritis. Its symptoms may be relieved, it may even go into periods of remission, but the unfortunate truth is that arthritis is incurable. Anyone promising a cure is a quack. As for pain and inflammation treatment, there are legitimate and illegitimate players in the field. Before you accept any treatment, be sure it has been approved by a reputable doctor.

Cancer: Victims and the families of victims of cancer are prime targets for quackery. Quackery thrives on the misfortune of others, and there are fewer misfortunes graver than a family member being stricken with cancer. People become so desperate they want to believe anything.

Quacks often hype "miracle machines" to cure cancer. Others fan the flames of paranoia and accuse the medical community of suppressing their cure and urge sufferers to leave the country to attend their clinics. Beware the cancer treatment that a reputable doctor refuses to administer to his or her patient.

Weight Loss: Who wouldn't like to be able to eat all they

want and still lose weight? Who wouldn't like to lose weight while they sleep? There's only one way to lose weight and that is to take in less calories than you expend whether through reducing your diet, increasing your exercise or both. Any "breakthrough" drug or weight loss tonic or device that claims otherwise is quacking up the wrong tree.

Impotency: Sexual dysfunction is very troubling. Its cause can be physical or psychological, but it can often be cured. However, it is not affected by "2000 year old powders that are not a drug or a hormone" as one bold advertisement once crowed (or quacked) or by any other mail order treatment. If you suffer from impotence, seek assistance from your doctor. If the problem is not physical, seek treatment from a licensed therapist trained in the treatment of sexual difficulties.

There is probably a quack scheme for every ailment known to man from hair loss to the common cold. The following are some of the more common promotional devices used by quacks to pull the wool over their victim's eyes:

Mail order offers with a money back guarantee: Too often your letter requesting a refund will be returned marked "return to sender."

Testimonials from "satisfied users": If they sound too good to be true, they usually are.

Promises of "quick and painless cures": Being cheated out of your money may be quick, but never painless.

Advertisements of "scientific breakthroughs" and "miracle cures" or "secret ancient formulas": The Food and Drug Administration and the Federal Trade Commission require proof that drugs and other forms of medical treatment really work before they permit them on the market. Once approved, such treatments will be administered by qualified health care professionals. Mail order or newspaper advertised treatments are usually not worth the paper they are printed on.

When it comes to your health, it is best to look before you leap. If you are interested in any health care product, call your trusted primary care physician and ask for his or her advice. Another person to consult is your pharmacist. If he or she cannot confirm the treatment, it is probably a scam.

BUSINESS OPPORTUNITY FRAUDS

The entrepreneurial spirit that made America great inspires many seniors to start a business even after retirement. Many start by investing in business opportunities, especially ones that can be operated part time or can be run from the home. All too often, the business opportunity of today turns into the nightmare of tomorrow.

According to the Economic Crime Project of the National District Attorney's Association, tens of thousands of people are cheated every year by con artists who promise the moon but deliver almost nothing. For example, the Economic Crime Project reports that an Iowa investor paid $5,490 for vending machines. The company promised to place the vending machines in busy locations and guaranteed an income of $42,000 a year. The reality was that the machines were scattered over 138 miles making them impossible to service and produced few sales and no profit.

Don't let that happen to you. Maximize your potential for success by being a smart consumer. Hire a business lawyer and/or a certified public accountant to assist you with the purchase. I mean, if you are going to lay your money down, at least have someone you can blame if things go wrong. An ounce of prevention is worth a pound of cure. A good lawyer will thoroughly investigate the books, claims and reputation of the proposed seller and tell you whether the contract of sale seems valid and what things you have to do if you go it on your own. Besides, a lawyer may be able to smell a rat when all you notice is the sweet scent of profit.

Beyond using your noodle when purchasing a business opportunity, know the Economic Crime Project's Warning Signs of Fraud:

—Undue pressure to sign a contract quickly and a demand to pay a large sum of money before sales claims can be investigated or legal advice obtained.

—Promises of extraordinarily high or guaranteed profits.

—Claims that profits can be achieved easily.

—A required initial fee which greatly exceeds the fair market value of any products, kits or training.

—A large fee payable before you receive anything in return.

—Evasive answers by the salesperson or unwillingness to give disclosure documents required by law.

Or to quote a great American truism, "There's no such thing as a free lunch."

SCAMS AND CON GAMES

Scams and con games can be the sources of great fun and entertainment when they are depicted Hollywood style in a movie like "The Sting." But when these crimes hit close to home, they cease to be fun and they are certainly not entertaining unless, of course, your idea of a good time happens to be devastated bank accounts and ruined lives.

Older people are the favorite targets of scam artists. According to the experts I interviewed, the reasons for this are:

—Older people find it harder to identify the perpetrator of the crime.

—Older people do not react as quickly to impropriety.

—Older people tend to stay in the con longer because they tend to be more trusting, especially of someone who appears trustworthy.

—Older people are generally more susceptible to pressure.

—Older people are more reluctant to say no.

—Once conned, older people are reluctant to come forward to report the crime. In fact, many keep the con a secret for fear that they will be thought senile or incapable of taking care of themselves. Forewarned is forearmed.

The word artist is particularly apt; these men and women are artists, dramatic actors who could put Sir Laurence Olivier to shame. The purpose behind their performance is to get you to trust them or feel sorry for them or otherwise persuade you that it is safe or right for you to give them your money, credit card number or other form of valuable property. You can't spot a con artist by his or her looks because they are deceiving.

But what kind of games do these villains play? While there are probably as many scams as there are con men and women willing to victimize the unwary, variations on the same con schemes are pulled over and over again. Here's a sampling:

The Pigeon Drop: In this famous scam, the "pigeon" or victim is approached by a con artist who shows him or her a large bundle of money. The con artist, in obvious distress, thinks the money is "hot" and asks for advice on what to do with it. At that moment, a second con walks up and acts like a stranger. The first con relates the story again. The cons suggest that the three divide the money after it has "cooled off." They also suggest that each contribute some of their own money to guarantee everyone will show up at the agreed time to make the division. The pigeon is chosen to keep the cash, which makes it even more tempting to get involved since he or she has nothing to lose, right? After all, the money will be safe with him or her. However, after everyone puts in their share of extra money, the cons turn a sleight of hand and take all the cash, leaving the "pigeon" unknowingly with an empty envelope.

The Bank Examiner Scheme: This racket has a phony bank examiner or other purported law enforcement officer contact the victim in search of assistance. The "officer" will probably be carrying "credentials" and he or she may even know the victim's account number having cased the "mark" before the scam starts. It seems that there is a crooked bank employee at the victim's bank, but they have not been able to catch this nefarious employee and need help. The victim is asked to go to the bank and withdraw a specified amount of money which they will in turn redeposit in the victim's account to make sure all of the paperwork is done correctly. The victim, eager to do his or her civic duty, does what is asked and turns the money over to the bank examiner. The bank examiner issues an official receipt, thanks the victim and is never heard from again. Needless to say, the money is never redeposited in the account.

The Pyramid Schemes: Every few years or so a new wave of pyramid schemes seems to sweep the country much like the regular invasion of Type A flu. And every time the pyramids appear, thousands of people rush to join with the result that they and others they bring into the scheme, friends or loved ones, lose their money.

Here's how a pyramid works: The mastermind offers "distributorships" or "shares" to six or so people for say $1,000 each. For the $1,000, each distributor is allowed to sell six further distributorships for $1,000. Of that sum, the mastermind keeps half and the distributor keeps half. Thus, the early distributors are even after selling two more distributorships and are turning a profit upon the sale of three. Each of these sub-distributors are then to go out and sell six more distributorships each and so on down the line. The mastermind is, of course, doing very well indeed—$1,000 per initial distributorship, $500 for each sale by the first distributors and $250 for each distributorhip the next level sells. Early participants can also do well, but there is no way to know how far up or down the line you are because at some point money goes in and never comes out.

The idea behind the pyramid scheme is to receive a lot of money without having to do any work. And as pitched by the charismatic mastermind, the pyramid does seem like a perpetual motion, money-making machine where everyone makes money, but no one gets hurt. Unfortunately, life just isn't that easy; the game can only go on for a short period of time because before long, a distributorship would have to be sold to every man, woman and child in the United States in order for it to continue, as illustrated below.

LEVEL	PARTICIPANTS
1	6
2	36
3	216
4	1,296
5	7,776
6	46,656
7	279,936
8	1,679,616
9	10,077,696
10	60,466,176
11	362,797,056—over 100 million more than the U.S. population

If you are approached to join a pyramid, just say no. Not only will you save yourself money, but also a lot of guilt since you won't have to watch the money of those you bring into the scheme going down the drain.

The Ponzi Scheme: The Ponzi scheme is named after its creator, Charles A. Ponzi, who cheated hundreds of investors in the 1920s. The scam is ingenious. The promoter, in the guise of a successful businessman, sets up a scam business and offers stock shares or other forms of investments, promising very high rates of return, about 20% within a month. A month later, son of a gun, the promoter says that business is good and he pays off!

"Oh boy!" says the investor, "I've struck it rich!" The

investor not only reinvests his or her earnings, but more money as well. In addition, friends are turned on to this fantastic investment opportunity (sometimes with commissions as incentives). Meanwhile, the promoter is living very well and paying the old investors a return with the money paid in by the new investors. The promoter will milk this sweet deal for all it is worth and then when new investment money slows or the cops seem to be closing in, he will pull the plug, and leave the investors holding an empty money bag.

Home Improvement Frauds: Many older people are bilked by home improvement scams. Typically, a salesman will come to the door soliciting home improvement work or advertisements may appear in the local newspaper offering senior citizen discounts. It may be for roofing, fixing water damage, repairing a fence or trimming the trees.

Once the victim expresses an interest, he or she is quickly pressured into signing a contract where a substantial down payment is required before work can begin. Sometimes the contractor simply keeps the money and never does the work. At other times, the work seems to be done and the victim pays the contract in full. The only problem is that a facade is just put on to make it look like real work was done. Thus, the leaky roof that was fixed during the summer still leaks in the winter. The driveway that was repaired turns out to only have been painted with an oily substance to look good.

The best way to fight this scam is to:

—Use only licensed and bonded contractors for your home improvement work. Also, be sure to check on the validity of the license with state agencies and the status of the bond with the bonding company.

—Get a lawyer to assist you in making the deal. Don't put a lot of money down. Rather, pay as the work is completed to your satisfaction.

—Get the name of five satisfied customers in your area and contact them as references;

—Visit the office of the contractor to make sure it is an established business.

—Never pay in cash.

If you succumb to a con or believe you are the target of a scam or fraud, contact the police authorities immediately. If the fraud is being perpetrated by mail, contact your nearest postmaster who will put you in touch with the postal inspectors. Do not keep quiet about what is going on. These thieves thrive on your silence and your embarrassment.

CRIMES OF VIOLENCE AND THEFT

Perhaps one of the greatest fears that seniors have is falling victim to a crime of violence or theft. These fears are not unfounded. Older people frequently are the targets of criminals who "earn" their living by attacking and/or stealing from others. Older people are less likely to defend themselves against an assailant who is younger and stronger.

That does not mean, however, that seniors are doomed to be hapless victims of circumstance. On the contrary, by taking common sense steps, the risks of becoming a crime statistic can be greatly reduced.

BURGLARY:

Burglary is the unlawful entrance into a building for a criminal purpose. Typically, a burglar enters a victim's home in order to steal property to be sold later for cash. Over six million residential burglaries occur every year. That's one every ten seconds!

The irony is that most burglaries can be prevented. For example, more than half of all residential burglaries occur without the criminal having to force his or her way in. In other words, they enter through unlocked doors or windows.

We've all heard the saying "the best defense is a good offense." Well, when it comes to preventing burglaries, the best defense is a good defense. Here are some tips to avoid burglaries:

—Always lock your doors and windows whenever you leave your home. Even if you are only going to be gone for a minute. It only takes that long for a crook to rush in and steal you blind.

—Never leave a housekey under the mat or in the flower pot by the front door. Those places are the first places a burglar looks.

—Exterior doors should have a deadbolt lock that extends into the doorframe. Simple pushbutton locks are almost useless except against the local toddler who mistakes your house for his or hers.

—Sliding doors and windows should have special locks installed. Another trick is to drill a hole through the door and metal frame and put in a thick screw.

—Be sure garage doors and gates are solidly locked.

—If you go out, use timers on the lights, radio and television set to go on and off at varied intervals to give the appearance that someone is home. If those aren't available, keep your radio on.

—If you are taking a long trip, be sure to halt mail and newspaper delivery and have a neighbor keep an eye on things. Newspapers and mail that aren't picked up are like gold-plated invitations to a burglary party.

—Install a wide angle lens viewer in the front door. Never open the door unless you know who is there.

—Identify your valuables by marking them with your driver's license number or date of birth. Marked items are worth less on the black market and may be left behind. Take pictures of all valuables you keep at home for insurance purposes. Better yet, don't keep valuables at home. Use a safe deposit box.

—Whenever you move to a new house, change the locks.

—Make sure your property is well-lit at night.

—Consider installing an alarm or a security service.

—OF SPECIAL IMPORTANCE—if you come home

and find the door open or other indications of forcible entry, do not go in the house! Most burglars do not want a confrontation, but may turn violent when cornered. No matter how valuable your property is, it's not worth your life or health.

If you are burglarized call the police. Your property may never be recovered, but you never know. Millions of dollars of unclaimed property is auctioned off each year by police agencies. Also, unless you report the crime, your insurance will not pay for your losses. Besides, even if the police have only a small chance of catching the crook, they will have absolutely no chance if you keep the crime to yourself.

ROBBERY AND THEFT:

Theft is the unlawful taking of another person's property. Robbery is the presence or threat of force in the commission of theft. Both thieves and robbers consider seniors easy prey; these villains tend to pick on those who are "asking" for trouble by the way they handle themselves.

Here are some tips to help you avoid being victimized:

—If you carry a purse, hold it close to your body—do not dangle it. To do otherwise is to invite pursesnatching.

—Never carry your wallet in your back pocket; put it in an inside jacket pocket or front pocket. Pickpockets love men who have wallet bulges in the seat of their pants.

—Make sure someone knows where you are going and when you can be expected to return.

—When using public transportation, sit near the driver.

—Don't travel dark or deserted routes. Don't travel alone if you can help it; there is safety in numbers.

—Have your key in hand as you approach your car or home.

—Do not carry so many packages that your view is obstructed and you are unable to react to danger.

—Carry a whistle or freon horn. Many community groups offer these devices free to seniors.

—Use travelers' checks instead of cash to minimize your

loss since you can receive compensation for lost or stolen travelers' checks.

—When you drive, keep your windows up and your doors locked. Park in well-lit areas and be wary of strangers asking for help. Instead, offer to call the police or a tow truck once you get home.

—If a friend or taxi drives you home, ask them to wait until you are safely inside before driving off.

—When walking, act calm and confident. Trust your gut feelings. If your internal danger alarm begins to sound, be extra careful.

If you are physically attacked, do not resist if the assailant is only after your purse. If you resist, chances are you will be hurt. Obviously, if the attack is more personal, defend yourself in any way that you can.

Many communities offer crime prevention programs such as Neighborhood Watch in California and Crimes Against Senior Citizens Squads in New York City. Ask your city council person's office for the details in your area. In addition, many states offer some form of assistance or compensation to the victims of crime, especially if they are violent. If you have been victimized, ask your local district attorney's office about the laws in your state. There are also many anti-crime and victim assistance programs established around the country. The following are two that are very vigorous in their work. You can contact them for more information.

Victims of Crime Resource Center   (916) 739-7049
McGeorge School of Law
University of the Pacific
3200 Fifth Avenue
Sacramento, CA 95817

National Organization for Victim Assistance
717 D St. N.W.
Washington D.C. 20004

9

We're Here To Help

The Professionals and Organizations That Assist Seniors

Community is a wonderful word that implies a cohesive group united by a sense of mutual trust and purpose. Within its scope can be found the idealistic concepts of giving, sharing and support. Community represents the best that we strive to be. But this sense of community does not happen by accident. In order to reach the ideal of community, all must labor long and hard in order to find common ground and forge the ties that bind.

Creating community for seniors has been no exception. It takes a lot of work to accomplish this worthy task. This chapter is about those organizations and professions who toil in this field.

AMERICAN ASSOCIATION OF RETIRED PERSONS

The American Association of Retired Persons (AARP) was formed in 1958 and in those thirty plus years, it has become one of the most powerful voices in the nation. Its motto is, "To serve, not be served." And serve, it does.

The AARP has the following stated goals:

—to enhance the quality of life for older persons;

—to promote independence, dignity and purpose for older persons;

—to lead in determining the role of older persons in society;

—to stimulate the private sector to support and pursue benevolent activities in the field of aging;

—to improve the image of aging.

The organization pursues these goals in so many ways that only one word does the AARP justice—awesome. The following programs and services may be of interest:

Information: The AARP publishes *The AARP News Letter* and *Modern Maturity Magazine. Modern Maturity* has the third largest circulation in the country (over 16 million). The purpose of *Modern Maturity* is to bring you information on matters ranging from health care to financial planning to living the good life in retirement. More good news; the magazine and newsletter are free to all members of the organization. *Modern Maturity* also comes in a televised format that can be seen around the country on many public broadcasting stations. There are also a series of AARP books to inform and enlighten.

Consumer Education: The AARP is on the frontlines when it comes to giving consumers the information they need to effectively purchase goods and services in the marketplace. Countless booklets have been published on topics ranging from methods to cut your phone costs to housing options for older Americans. For a complete list of these educational pamphlets, contact your local chapter.

Services: AARP provides many services designed to save precious time and money for its members. These include the

AARP Pharmacy, the largest nonprofit mail service pharmacy in the world, the AARP Investment Program and the AARP Motoring Plan, an emergency roadside service. In addition, the AARP offers a travel service, group health insurance and homeowners insurance programs.

> **NOTE:** Many of these services are operated through private companies that contract with the AARP to offer their wares to members. Treat the services offered as you would any other purveyor. In other words, shop around and compare before you put your money down.

Programs: The AARP's educational and service programs reach people of all ages throughout the country. Program topics include the Institute of Lifetime Learning, that assists in developing the opportunity for older Americans to enjoy continuing educational activities; the Health Advocacy Series, that seeks to promote good health practices and Reminiscence, a program that trains volunteers to visit isolated seniors and share their memories. There is also the Widowed Persons Service; Traffic and Driver Safety and Tax-Aide, just to mention a few.

Foundations: The Andrus Foundation awards grants and educational assistance to universities that engage in research in the field of gerontology.

Volunteers: The AARP has several volunteer programs available to any member who wishes to pitch in. Much of the work is run out of the 3,500 local chapters around the country. However, there is also a national volunteer network of more than 6,000 officials divided into ten areas throughout the country. In addition, volunteers throughout the country serve as lobbyists for seniors by keeping on top of legislation offered nationally and throughout the 50 states.

Advocacy: The term, "special interest," has gotten a poor reputation in recent years. But seniors are special and they have the right to persuade a representative government to address their concerns. The AARP performs this function so well that it has become one of the most powerful advocacy forces in the country today.

If you are age 50 or over, I urge you to join. The cost is only five dollars. If you are interested in joining or would like more information, the national address for the AARP is:

AARP National Headquarters
1909 K St. N.W.
Washington D.C. 20049

(The address and phone numbers of all area offices can be found in the supplement at the end of this book.)

There's just one more thing to remember: WHEN IN DOUBT, CALL THE AARP.

NATIONAL COUNCIL OF SENIOR CITIZENS

Like the AARP, the National Council of Senior Citizens serves as an advocate for and benefactor of seniors and their families. The NCSC offers several programs such as The Nursing Home Information Service. It also publishes a number of informational pamphlets that assist elders and their families. Other benefits available to the four million members of this fine organization are insurance and health plans as well as recreation and travel discounts.

There is no age restriction for joining, so families of older citizens can join along with their parents or loved ones. Of course, like the AARP, it can get expensive. After all, eight dollars doesn't exactly grow on trees.

If you are interested in more information about the National Council of Senior Citizens, write or call:

National Council of Senior Citizens
925 15th Street N.W.
Washington D.C. 20005
(202) 347-8800

NATIONAL INSTITUTE ON AGING

In 1974, the Research on Aging Act was signed into law, thereby establishing the National Institute On Aging (NIA) to "conduct and support biomedical, social and behavioral research and training related to the aging process and the diseases and other special problems and needs of the aging."

In the short years since the NIA was established, a number of findings were reported by Institute scientists and researchers. Among them were:

—Older cells reproduce at a lower rate than younger cells. This means that healing and immune functions (the ability to resist disease) may operate less efficiently in older people.

—Healthy older men maintain their production of sex hormones at levels found in younger men.

—If it is free of disease, the heart of an older person appears to pump about as well as that of a young adult. Thus, any problems related to the older heart's ability to move blood may be considered the effect of disease, not aging.

—Contrary to traditional beliefs, a long-term study revealed that at all ages the majority of people maintain or actually improve their levels of intellectual competence as they grow older.

—Problems such as cardiovascular disease and disadvantaged socioeconomic conditions can undermine intellectual abilities.

—While aging undermines physical strength and motor performance, exercise can counteract some of these effects. Experiments indicate that tissues of aging hearts in animals benefit significantly from moderate exercise.

These and many other findings and conclusions resulting from NIA conducted and sponsored research has enabled health and geriatric professionals to provide better and more complete care for older people. That alone is no small achievement. But there's more. Realizing that knowledge is power, the NIA also offers many publications on topics of great concern and interest to our older citizens, such as "Q & A: Alzheimer's Disease" and "Safe Use of Medicines By Older People" bring needed knowledge and information to seniors and their families as they adjust to the problems and joys of life in the golden years.

For more information on aging or on other NIA programs and information packets, contact:

NIA Information Center
2209 Distribution Circle
Silver Springs, MD 20910
(301) 495-3455

NATIONAL SENIOR CITIZENS LAW CENTER

There are few who would dispute the importance of having a good lawyer in time of legal need. Unfortunately, most of the good lawyers are expensive, thereby supporting the truism that in our adversary system, justice all too often goes to the highest bidder.

The purpose behind the National Senior Citizens Law Center is to equalize the playing field when it comes to law, the courts and government programs. The emphasis is on assisting senior citizens of limited incomes. The hope is that by acting as legal advocates for these Americans, all seniors can live their lives in dignity and freedom from poverty.

NSCLC attorneys specialize in priority areas having frequent impact on the elderly poor. Among these areas and staff specialties are the following:

Social Security and Supplemental Security Income: Whether it is helping combat improper refusal or termination of benefits or testifying before Congress and regulatory agencies, the NSCLC fights the good fight for seniors who might otherwise have to go it alone.

Medicare: Likewise, NSCLC assists Medicare recipients who are having problems with Part A benefits, including DRG disputes and Part B difficulties, such as a disagreement over the reasonable value of a service rendered. Consumer information about Medicare issues is also available.

Nursing Home Residents' Rights: Technical and strategic assistance is given in patient transfer cases and with litigation in issues over quality of care. The center also assists other attorneys and professionals in the field by publishing the "Nursing Home Law Letter."

Pensions: The Center provides litigation and other forms of assistance regarding retirees' claims for private and public pension benefits. Special emphasis is placed on securing the rights guaranteed under ERISA (Employee Retirement Security Act) as well as the Railroad Retirement Act and federal civil service issues substituting for ERISA controversies.

Age Discrimination: NSCLC works to implement the rights guaranteed to older Americans by the Age Discrimination Act of 1975. It also comes to the assistance of workers who have been victims of mass layoffs and plant closings.

NSCLC's primary method of rendering assistance is to support attorneys working in center field programs. However, if you have a problem not covered by the NSCLC that involves the legal rights of seniors, you and/or your lawyer can still receive technical assistance in support of your cause.

For further information contact the NSCLC at either of the following locations:

1052 W. 6th Street
Los Angeles, CA. 90017
(213) 482-3550

2025 M Street, N.W.
Washington D.C. 20036
(202) 887-5280

> **NOTE:** The NSCLC does not usually get involved in matters such as landlord tenant disputes, civil cases or other areas of the law that are not primarily related to older Americans. If you have such a problem and cannot afford to hire a lawyer, contact your local Legal Aid office or local bar association many of which offer low cost or free legal services to needy litigants.

HEALTH FOUNDATIONS

As discussed in Chapter 3, there are many nonprofit organizations and foundations whose function is to assist seniors (and others) who suffer from specific ailments. The American Heart Association and the American Cancer Society are just two of the more famous examples of such groups.

Virtually all of these various and sundry organizations offer information and practical assistance to sufferers of the malady each organization is concerned with. Some also offer financial assistance to those needing special care.

Most of these organizations have chapters in most major cities. If you or a loved one has been diagnosed as suffering from a malady and you want to know whether there is an organization or foundation to assist you, ask your physician, contact your local medical society or inquire at the gerontology center nearest you.

OLDER WOMEN'S LEAGUE

The Older Women's League, as the name implies, is the first national grassroots membership organization to focus exclusively on women as they age. The purposes of OWL are to provide mutual support for its members, to help women achieve economic and social equity and to improve the image and status of older women.

This is not a trivial undertaking. According to OWL:

—over 70% of people over the age of 65 are women;

—fewer than one woman in five over the age of 65 receives pension income;

—85% of all surviving spouses over the age of 65 are women;

—80% of the elderly who live alone are women.

OWL works through local chapters to assist its members with these and other difficult life issues and to plan better for the latter stages of adult life. This is accomplished through workshops, the distribution of educational materials and the development of model state laws to alleviate problems of older women. OWL offers group insurance benefits and other perks of membership. Joining will cost you the sum total of $10.

To see whether there is an OWL chapter in your neck of the woods, contact:

Older Women's League
730 Eleventh St. N.W.
Suite 300
Washington D.C. 20001
(202) 783-6686

GRAY PANTHERS

The Gray Panthers are a national organization of over 60,000 activists who work for political change, particularly in the areas of peace, health care and aging. As an activist organization, the Gray Panthers often organize letter writing and lobbying campaigns concerning issues affecting membership's interests. In addition, local chapters can be relied upon as referral guides to local senior assistance resources.

If you have any questions about the Gray Panthers and/or the location of local chapters, contact:

Gray Panthers
311 S. Juniper St., Suite 601
Philadelphia, PA 19107
(215) 545-6555

HEALTH CARE PROFESSIONALS

When we think of health care professionals, we usually think of medical doctors. But doctors are only part, albeit a very important part, of your health care team. The most important thing you can do for yourself vis-a-vis doctors is to find and keep a good primary care physician who takes an active interest in treating seniors. Beyond these very important doctors are sub-specialists who are experts in specific areas of medicine. Here is just a partial list:

Sub-specialists Of Internal Medicine: The internist is a doctor who practices in the field of internal medicine. Some internists go on to sub-specialize, that is, they leave the field of general care to focus on a limited area of the body. This is accomplished by continuing training in residency beyond what is required to become an internist. These sub-specialties are:

—Cardiology—the treatment of the heart and vascular

system (blood vessels). Remember, since cardiologists are internists, they do not perform surgery.

—Endocrinology—the treatment of metabolic diseases such as diabetes.

—Gastroenterology—a field concerned with the diseases of the digestive system.

—Hematology—the treatment of afflictions and diseases of the blood.

—Infectious Disease—which deals with afflictions caused by microorganisms such as bacterial infections.

—Oncology—the treatment of cancer.

—Nephrology—the treatment of diseases of the kidneys.

—Pulmonary Disease—the treatment of diseases of the lungs.

—Rheumatology—the treatment of arthritis.

Surgeons: In a way, the field of surgery is very much like the field of internal medicine. The similarity is in the sub-specialty system. There are general surgeons and then there are sub-specialists who train intensely in restricted fields.

General surgeons perform general abdominal operations, lumpectomies, breast surgery and a wide variety of other procedures. The sub-specialties of the field include:

—Head and Neck Surgery—(formerly called ear, nose and throat) deals with surgery of the head and neck.

—Neurosurgery—surgery involving the brain, such as the removal of a tumor.

—Orthopedics—operations on bones and joints, such as a hip replacement. If you have serious arthritis of the hip, you would see a rheumatologist. But if he or she believed that a hip replacement was necessary, you would make that decision in consultation with an orthopedist who would perform the operation if you decided to proceed.

—Plastic Surgery—also known as reconstructive surgery, plastic surgery involves the repair of injured or deformed body parts, as well as the more commonly known cosmetic surgeries such as "chin tucks" and "face peels."

—Thoracic Surgery—surgery of the lungs and heart.

—Vascular Surgery—surgery of the blood vessels, such as the heart bypass.

> **NOTE:** Your primary physician knows best whether you should consult a surgeon, and if so, which one would be right for you. Surgery is best decided among the three of you, with a second and/or third opinion thrown in, just to be sure.

Gynecology: Just because a woman passes her childbearing years, doesn't mean she has no further use of a gynecologist to call her own. Women frequently have the need of treatment for matters such as cysts and fibroid tumors and other female problems even though they have passed menopause.

Urology: Many consider urologists to be the male equivalent of the gynecologist. This is an erroneous presumption. While it is true that urologists treat male problems such as prostate malfunction, they also treat diseases of the urinary tract in both genders and perform surgery.

Psychiatry: Psychiatrists are M.D.s who treat behavioral disorders of the mind. Many are beginning to emphasize treating mental diseases of older Americans.

Anesthesiology: Most people think of anesthesiologists as the doctor who puts you to sleep when you have surgery. They do administer the drugs that kill pain so that pain doesn't kill you in surgery, but they do much more than that. They are responsible for keeping you alive during the procedure.

Now that you have been introduced to the various doctors that typically treat older people, the next question is, "What do I look for in a doctor?" Well, my advice is to find a doctor who best meets the five As of medical criteria:

Ability   Affordability
Availability   Affability
Accessibility

Ability is obviously the most important of the five As. After all, the most affable doctor in the world who doesn't know that the "hipbone's connected to the thigh bone" isn't going to do you much good. Ability means that the doctor knows his or her stuff. It is usually illustrated by credentials, such as board certification and staffing privileges at the best hospitals.

Availability means that the doctor practices medicine in such a way that he or she will be there in time of need. Thus, a doctor who acts like the old Jack Benny joke about the Beverly Hills Police Department not being available because "they have an unlisted phone number" is not a good doctor for you even if he or she is the most capable in your city.

Accessibility is the ease with which you can get to your doctor's office. If you must take a bus and the doctor's office is 15 blocks from the bus stop, all of the doctor's ability is of little use to you if you are unable to make it to the office from the bus. Likewise, if money is a concern and the doctor doesn't validate parking, that $10 to park may keep you at home when you should be seeing your doctor.

Affordability, as you would expect, has to do with your ability to pay for the doctor of your choice. This can be a very real issue when you depend on Medicare. A capable doctor who refuses to accept the Medicare assignment (see Chapter 4) may just be too expensive, regardless of his or her credentials.

Affability deals with that art of medicine known as the bedside manner. The best doctor in theory, who is unable to communicate with you effectively, may not be the best doctor in practice.

Obviously, few doctors make a perfect score in each of the Five As. Some may be more important to you than others. For example, affability may mean more to you in your primary care physician than it does in your anesthesiologist, who will have much less direct contact with you. It is up to you to weigh the pros and cons of each and decide which doctor gives you the best combination of these attributes.

NURSES:

One of the most important but least appreciated member of your health care team is the nurse. If you are in the hospital and need hands-on attention, a nurse is there. If you've been in an accident and are rushed to the hospital by paramedics, a nurse is there directing your care by radio. If you need special care at home because you are too ill to take care of yourself but not ill enough to be hospitalized, a nurse is there. In fact, to paraphrase a quote from Churchill, rarely in the course of human services have so many been indebted to so few.

Nurses are better trained and perform more diverse services for their patients than ever before. Here is just a partial list of what the members of this dedicated profession do for us:

Registered Nurses: When most people think of nurses, they think of the hard working R.N. who can be found in hospitals, in doctor's offices, as part of home health care associations and everywhere nursing services are needed. R.N.s have tremendous responsibility placed on their shoulders including:

—Carrying out the medical regimen such as giving pills, administering injections, changing dressings, etc.

—Assisting the patient's emotional adjustment to his or her malady or life situation both in a hospital setting and at home.

—Educating the patient and his or her family in the skills of self-care.

—Acting as a "fail-safe" and alerting doctors to mistakes or problems that may be occurring during the patient's course of treatment, even though this mean confronting a doctor who is not performing up to par.

—Coordinating the medical team such as social worker, dietician and chaplain when patient care problems are discovered.

Nurse Practitioner: Nurse Practitioners generally have a masters degree and are permitted to give physical exams, order and interpret tests and treat common illnesses. In some states they are even permitted to prescribe medications. NPs generally manage "well" health care (checkups, monitoring chronic conditions, etc.) and can frequently be found in HMOs, outpatient clinics and as the assistant of a private practice physician. Many nurse practitioners sub-specialize in geriatric care.

Licensed Vocational Nurses: LVNs are the foot soldiers of health care. In other words, they perform the dirtiest tasks and receive the least credit of the professionals who work in the health care field. They also perform varied chores which make life more comfortable for patients, usually under the direction of an R.N.

PHARMACISTS:

Another underappreciated member of your dedicated health care team is your local pharmacist who dispenses the drugs prescribed to you by your physician and acts as your eyes and ears to make sure no mistakes are made.

This is far more important than it may initially appear. An unfortunate fact of life is that doctors and their staffs will sometimes drop the ball. These mistakes may come in the choice of medication or perhaps in the dosage of a proper prescription. Pharmacists serve as important double checkers of your doctor's prescribed plan of care. It is their job to catch any blunders that occur before they can cause you any trouble.

Another important function of the pharmacist is the prevention of accidental mismatching of prescribed drugs. Mismatching can occur when two or more doctors prescribe medications for different ailments which may be fine by themselves but which could create a toxic effect when taken together. Such mistakes are not uncommon with older patients who are likely to have more than one doctor treating them. By filling all of your drug needs with the same pharmacist, he or she is likely to catch mismatching before the mismatching catches you.

There are other things your pharmacist can do for you which can save you time, money and/or convenience.

—Your pharmacist (in cooperation with your doctor) can tell you whether generic drugs are appropriate in your case in place of the more expensive brand names.

—Your pharmacist can answer important information about your prescription which your doctor may not know or may not take the time to answer. He or she can tell you what to do if you miss a dose or how alcohol effects the drug's action. He or she can tell you about any side effects to watch out for and if the medicine comes in a more convenient form (such as a patch in place of pills). If you've got a question about your medication, your pharmacist should have the answer.

—Many pharmacies deliver at little or no charge which can be very important if you suffer from a disability.

—Many pharmacists offer senior citizen discounts which can add up to big bucks saved for you to enjoy.

—If you are having a side effect from a medication, call your doctor. If he or she isn't available, call your pharmacist.

—Your pharmacist can steer you toward beneficial over-the-counter medicines and away from those that are worthless or even harmful.

PRIVATE GERIATRIC CARE MANAGERS

As has been stated throughout this book, life for seniors in the last decade of the twentieth century is different from what it was for seniors of previous generations. For the most part, this has been positive. I mean, who can imagine a time without the benefits of social security and Medicare?

Just the same, many seniors simply do not receive the tender loving care that their forbearers used to receive from family and community. This is true for many reasons:

—The nuclear family (sons, daughters, spouse) is smaller than it used to be. Today, all or most of the family members work or are otherwise unable to devote a great deal of time to taking care of Mom or Dad when they can no longer completely take care of themselves. Moreover, children frequently live hundreds or even thousands of miles from their parents and are unavailable to provide much personal assistance to their parents in the event of need.

—The extended family (uncles, aunts, brothers, sisters, etc.) is also smaller and is often spread across the country. The valuable assistance that these relatives once gave to a caregiver is no longer available.

—People live longer than they used to. This has created a greater need for extended care than generally used to be the case.

—Hospitals are discharging older patients sicker and sooner as part of the cost effective solutions to the health care financial crunch of the 70s and 80s. This means that many older people require at least temporary assistance in living their lives.

—Culturally, the U.S.A. does not give the respect and reverence to the older generation that other countries do.

These "facts of life" have created the need for a recourse to assist families in assisting their older members. This need has given rise to what I call the "newest profession," the private geriatric care manager. The private geriatric care manager has several jobs, all of which may be vital to the health and well being of the senior in need.

Assessment of the needs of the parents and the caregiver. When a senior loses his or her ability to live a completely independent life, a crisis generally develops within the family of the person needing care. If a geriatric care manager is called to assist in the case, one of the initial jobs is to evaluate the total picture in order to come up with solutions that will be acceptable to the entire family. In other words, the solution must work for everyone or eventually it will work for no one.

Referrals to service providers. As you have learned in this book, there is an abundance of services available to assist seniors and their families in need. The problem is that many people don't always know what services are available in each locality and which providers are the best in town. One important job of the geriatric care manager is to find out what is available and to steer his or her clients to those service providers which give the most and best for the senior in need of assistance.

Referrals to professionals. Older people frequently have needs to be filled by professionals such as lawyers, doctors and psychotherapists. The good care manager should have a stable of good qualified professionals to whom they can refer their client.

Placement into appropriate residential facilities. It is often not difficult to figure out when an older person can no longer live a completely free and independent life. At such times, thoughts reluctantly turn to nursing homes. But there is a very large gray area between the freedom of independent life and the confinement of care in a nursing home. Knowing just where the older person's needs are within that spectrum is difficult. One of the jobs the care manager performs is to find the right spot and effect a placement, always with an eye to maintaining the maximum independence appropriate to the circumstances.

Provider of ombudsman services. A good private geriatric

care manager also acts as his or her client's advocate with the service providers recommended to the family. For instance, if the geriatric care manager places the client in a board and care home and the client is unhappy with the food, the care manager will step in to mediate and resolve the dispute.

Educator concerning issues of aging. The geriatric care manager must continually update him or herself on the issues of the aging and communicate what has been learned to his or her clients.

A friend to a friend in need. Frequently, care workers do what the children or other loved ones of a needy older person would do if they were there to do it. This might mean a regular visit to the client in the nursing home or a daily handholding phone call. It might mean following an Alzheimer's victim as he or she slowly grows worse so that the needs of the client can continually be upgraded to meet the developing condition. In short, the geriatric care manager fills the needs of those seniors who have been left high and dry in need of a friend.

There is no specific licensing in the geriatric care field. These care managers come from a wide variety of professions such as nursing, social work, marriage and family therapy or psychology. All charge for their services which is usually not paid for by health insurance.

There is a national organization if you would like more information or a referral to a care worker near you or your loved one. It is the National Association of Private Care Managers and its address is:

National Association of Private Care Managers
Box 6920
Yorkville Financial Station
New York, NY 10128

10

Everybody Loves Somebody Sometime

The Problems Faced By Senior Caregivers

Caring For An Older Relative In Your Own Home;
Services Available For Caregivers; ECHO
Housing; Nursing Home Care; Nursing Home
Patients' Rights; Nursing Home Checklist; Solving
Problems; Special Problems Of Alzheimer Disease
Victims, Caregivers

Behind those beautiful words pledging lifelong love lies a mountain of commitment. One such commitment is having to care for a spouse who can no longer care for him or herself. But how can one do that effectively when the caregiver is also a senior citizen?

Quid pro quo is a Latin phrase meaning to give in return for something given. For those of us with elderly parents, quid pro quo becomes a burning issue. After all, they gave us their all when we needed them. Now that they need us, do we become their primary caregivers? If so, what does it mean to our lives and the lives of the members of our own families?

Millions of seniors need some form of caregiver support in their later years. But just because these elders have reached a time when they cannot live independently does not mean that their lives cannot be happy and fulfilling. Likewise, people who love enough to take on the immense and sometimes thankless job of senior caregiving need not feel that their lives have to be diminished by the responsibilities they have assumed. Changed, yes. Made more complicated, definitely. But diminished? No. For in truth, caring for those we love can be one of life's most rewarding, if sometimes frustrating, experiences.

CARING IN YOUR OWN HOME

Most caregivers try to render their services in the home. If the caregiver is a spouse, the effort will be to keep the loved one at home in familiar environs for as long as possible. If the caregiver is a child, he or she may decide to bring the parent home. Either way, here are some things that caregivers need to be aware of:

THE TYPES OF SERVICES:

As we have discussed throughout this book, there are many services which are available to make the lives of seniors more enjoyable. These services and others are also available to caregivers in order to help them whenever possible and to reduce their own level of frustration.

Respite Care: Those caring for the most dependent seniors, such as Alzheimer's Disease victims (see below), will sometimes need a breather. This breather is called respite and is most commonly used by bringing a care helper into the home to care for the dependent senior while the caregiver goes out for a little recreation or to run errands. The respite time may be short, perhaps a few hours a day once or twice a week, or it may be longer, such as a weekend while the caregiver gets away for some well earned "R and R." In-home respite providers may be friends or community volunteers who help free of charge, or they may be paid professionals who charge a fee. Whatever the case, if you are an in-home caregiver, take advantage of home respite as often as you need to. After all, no one expects you to be superman or superwoman.

Respite care can also be given out of the home in day care centers. Day care centers are especially important for working caregivers for they allow the caregiver to go to work away from home with the peace of mind that their loved dependent senior is being well cared for. There are also board and care homes and nursing homes that will accept responsibility for a dependent senior for days or even weeks should the need arise. If you do intend to leave your loved one in your care of such a facility, make sure they are sufficiently equipped to handle your loved one's needs. If the older person you care for can't take care of his or her own hygiene, the care facility will have to have trained personnel available to help them out.

Homemaker Services: When you take on the added responsibility of caring for someone who simply cannot care for themselves, the little things such as washing floors and doing laundry can seem like monumental chores. If you can afford to bring in help to assist with these chores of daily living, you will be doing yourself a very big favor. Many home health care agencies offer homemaking services on a sliding scale based on ability to pay. So, even if your name isn't Donald Trump, you may be able to afford this very necessary help.

Home Health Care: Many seniors who require a caregiver's assistance also need continuing medical care. If you are going to keep your loved one out of a nursing home, you must learn to: a) give the medical care yourself (where appropriate), b) bring in home health care services, or c) all of the above. Limited financial resources need not necessarily be a problem because many nonprofit agencies in the field are willing to give you a break. In addition, some home nursing may be paid for under limited circumstances by Medicare.

Transportation Programs: One of the burdens of caring for a needy senior may be the time involved in getting them to needed doctor's appointments, to day care or senior centers, etc. Fortunately, most communities have transportation programs which can help your relatively able senior get around town without having to disrupt your work or daily routine.

Hospice Care: If you are caring for a senior with a terminal illness, definitely avail yourself of the services of a hospice to assist you and your loved one during this deeply emotional and trying time. Money should not be a factor since Medicare pays for hospice care.

For more information on these services, contact your local health care agencies, public health departments, churches, day care centers, area agencies on aging or a private geriatric case worker.

The services are designed to make your life as a caregiver easier. Here are some hints to help you make your home more comfortable:

—If possible, provide the older person with his or her own room or space where they can spend time in private. Ideally, the room should be on the first floor to avoid the necessity of climbing stairs.

—Encourage your senior to participate in home life, including chores, as much as physically possible.

—See to it that your loved one has a social life as health permits. Senior centers in your area should be consulted to see what programs are available.

—Install safety fixtures such as handrails next to the toilet and shower. A bench should also be put in the bathtub for easy and safe access.

—Install wrist straps on the walker or cane to reduce the chances of a fall.

—Remove all shag carpets and throw rugs to prevent slipping.

—If the person has physical difficulties, think about renting a hospital bed to make getting out of bed easier. Installing siderails will prevent him or her from falling out of bed.

Beyond the above, be sure to take the time to nourish yourself. It's not easy watching someone you love experience physical or mental difficulties. Be sensitive to signs of your own burnout such as impatience and irritation directed at the person in your care or other members of your family. Reach out to a friend, a mental health professional, your clergyman or a relative for assistance. Make a point of getting away now and then, even if it means placing your loved senior in a nursing home for a week or so. The sanity you save may be your own.

A NOTE ABOUT ECHO HOUSING:

Children of aging parents frequently want to bring them home to live but don't have the space. This problem may be solved by looking into ECHO (Elder Cottage Housing Opportunity) housing units. ECHO houses are factory built, self-contained living units that are designed to be installed in a yard for long-term use.

The wonderful part of ECHO housing is that it allows the senior to live independently in a detached living space while being only a stone's throw away from family. This helps the older person remain independent while allowing the caring family to maintain privacy. Also, since the cottages are not permanent structures (although they are as just as comfortable), when the senior no longer is using the facility, it can be disassembled and the yard can be returned to its former state.

ECHO housing is definitely an idea whose time has come but there are some problems:

Cost: Not everyone can afford the $16,000-$25,000 price tag which includes items such as foundation, water, sewer and electrical hook-up but not landscaping and site drainage.

(Prices are subject to change and may vary in different regions of the country.)

Zoning: Many communities frown on building additional structures in the yards of single family residences and have zoning laws that discourage or prohibit ECHO housing. However, since these laws were not aimed at preventing families from caring for their elderly relatives, many communities are easing restrictions permitting zoning variances for the installation of an elder cottage.

Space: Despite the fact that elder cottages are not large (ranging from 288 sq. feet to 720 sq. feet), they are large enough to prevent their use in small yards.

If you would like more information about ECHO housing, please contact:

> Coastal Colonial Corporation
> Box 452-A, R.D. 4
> Manheim, PA 17545
> (717) 665-6761

NURSING HOME CARE

There may come a time when, for whatever reasons, an older person simply must be placed in a long-term nursing care facility commonly known as a nursing home. The decision to take this step is never an easy one. Nursing homes have the sometimes deserved reputation as being places where seniors are warehoused rather than provided with quality custodial care. However, there are an abundance of nursing homes that do provide excellent care.

The problem, of course, is to find them. After all, most of us don't spend our spare hours boning up on the ins and outs of nursing home care. When the time of need arises we are usually in a crisis situation which is less than an opportune time to make such an important decision.

UNDERSTAND WHAT YOU ARE PAYING FOR:
Nursing homes provide four basic services:

—Medical care is usually provided by the patient's own doctor who admits his or her patient to the nursing home and who remains personally responsible for the patient's continuing medical treatment.

—Nursing care by RNs and LVNs, such as administering medicine, injections, catheterizations, etc. as ordered by a doctor.

—Personal care, such as assistance in walking, bathing, eating, dressing and the preparation of special diets as ordered by a physician.

—Residential services including general supervision and protection, room and board, and a program of social and recreational activities.

The level and quality of services will vary from nursing home to nursing home. You want a home that provides the best mix of services to meet your loved one's needs both at the time of admission and if his or her condition worsens.

PLAN AHEAD:
If you are the caregiver for a senior, it is not disloyal to look into your community's nursing homes in advance of need. In that way you will have the luxury of time to find those homes which can best care for your loved one should you no longer be able to.

KNOW THE RIGHTS OF NURSING HOME PATIENTS:
Many states have laws which guarantee the rights of nursing home patients. When looking into nursing facilities, make sure that the administrators take the following patients' rights seriously:

—the right to safe considerate care;

—an environment which is clean, sanitary and in good repair;

—a diet consisting of a variety of good quality foods as prescribed by the patient's physician;

—the presence of organized activities;

—the right to privacy when visited by a spouse and the right to share a room if both spouses are residents of the facility;

—liberal visiting hours on a daily basis;

—an environment in which grievances may be presented without fear of reprisal;

—dignity and respect in personal care;

—an environment which allows freedom of religious expression and worship;

—an opportunity for the patient to purchase drugs and medical supplies from a pharmacy or other source of their choice.

CHECK THE COST:

Different nursing homes offer various prices for their services ranging from expensive to exorbitant except, in very limited circumstances, you will receive absolutely no assistance in paying for this cost from Medicare. Thus, the patient or the family will be responsible for paying the $35 to $100 plus per day cost of care.

The reality of these circumstances is that many nursing home patients are literally pauperized paying for care. This fact of life compels the caregiver to look into how the bills will be paid (such as half by the patient and half by the family) and into legal/financial planning and alternate sources of financing such as insurance, Medicaid and veteran's benefits.

CHECK THE LOCATION:

One of the best ways to ensure that your loved one receives top-notch care is to visit, visit and then visit again. In order to do this frequently, you should find a good nursing home that is relatively close to you.

CHECK THE FACILITIES:

When you are choosing a nursing home, you should compare and contrast facilities just as you would when choosing any product or service. Use the following guidelines prepared by the Department of Health Services for the County of Los Angeles which raises the important issues and asks most of the questions you want answered when choosing a nursing home:

Is the home certified to participate in the Medicare and Medicaid programs? (This is vital since patients in uncertified homes are probably not eligible to receive benefits.)

Does the nursing home have all necessary state licenses?

Is the most recent licensing report posted in a prominent location? (The licensing report will outline problems that were found in the last inspection.)

Does the administrator have a current license?

Does the home provide special services (such as rehabilitation therapy, diet, etc.) that the patient requires?

Is the general atmosphere of the nursing home warm, pleasant and cheerful?

Are the administrator and staff cheerful, enthusiastic and genuinely interested in their patients?

Do the residents look well cared for and generally content?

Are residents allowed to wear their own clothes, decorate their own rooms and keep a few prized possessions on hand?

Is there a place for private family visits?

Do residents, other visitors and volunteers speak favorably about the home?

GENERAL PHYSICAL CONSIDERATIONS

Is the nursing home clean and orderly?

Is the home reasonably free from unpleasant odors?

Are rooms well ventilated and kept at a comfortable temperature?

SAFETY

Are wheelchair ramps provided where necessary?

Is the nursing home free of obvious hazards, such as obstacles under foot and unsteady furniture?

Are there grab bars in toilet and bathing facilities and handrails on both sides of hallways?

Do bathtubs and showers have nonslip surfaces?

Are there portable fire extinguishers?

Are there smoke detectors, an automatic sprinkler system and automatic emergency lighting?

Are exits clearly marked and exit signs illuminated?

Are exit doors unobstructed and unlocked from inside?

Are certain areas posted with no smoking signs and are these restrictions enforced?

Is an emergency evacuation plan posted in prominent locations?

MEDICAL, DENTAL AND OTHER SERVICES

Does the home have an arrangement with an outside dental service to provide patients with dental care when necessary?

In case of medical emergencies, is a physician available at all times, either on staff or on call?

Does the home have arrangements with a nearby hospital for quick transfer of nursing home patients in an emergency?

Is emergency transportation readily available?

PHARMACEUTICAL SERVICES

Are pharmaceutical services supervised by a qualifed pharmacist?

Is a room set aside for storing and preparing drugs?

Does a qualified pharmacist maintain and monitor a record of each patient's drug therapy?

Does the facility encourage the purchase of drugs from the supplier of your choice?

NURSING SERVICES

Is at least one registered nurse or licensed vocational nurse on duty day and night?

Are nurse or emergency call buttons located at each patient's bed and in toilet and bathing facilities?

Is an R.N. on duty during the day, seven days a week?

FOOD SERVICES

Is the kitchen clean and reasonably tidy? Is proper refrigeration available? Is waste properly disposed of?

Ask to see the meal schedule. Are at least three meals served each day? Are meals served at normal hours, with plenty of time left for eating leisurely?

Are nutritious between-meal snacks available?

Are patients given enough food? Does the food appear to be appetizing? (Why not taste the food yourself?)

Does the meal being served match the posted menu?

Are special meals prepared for residents who are restricted to special diets?

Is the dining room attractive and comfortable?

Is there assistance available for those patients who need help in eating?

SOCIAL SERVICES AND PATIENT ACTIVITIES

Are there social services available to aid patients and their families?

Does the nursing home have a varied program of recreational, cultural and intellectual activities for patients?

Is there an activities director on the staff?

Are activities offered for patients who are relatively inactive or confined to their rooms?

Look at the activities schedule. Are some activities scheduled in the evenings?

PATIENTS' ROOMS
Does each room open into a hallway?

Does each room have a window?

Does each patient have a reading light, a comfortable chair, a closet and drawers for personal belongings?

Is there fresh drinking water within reach?

Is there a curtain or screen available to provide privacy for each bed whenever necessary?

Do bathing and toilet facilities have adequate privacy?

OTHER AREAS OF THE NURSING HOME
Is there a lounge where patients can chat, read, play games, watch television or just relax away from their rooms?

Is there a public telephone available for patients' use?

Does the nursing home have an outdoor area where patients can get fresh air and sunshine?

FINANCIAL AND RELATED MATTERS
Do the estimated monthly costs, including extra charges, compare favorably with the cost of other homes?

Is a refund made for unused days paid for in advance?

Will the nursing home allow the patient to remain in the facility after he or she exhausts private funds and becomes eligible for Medicaid? (If not, you will have to move the patient to another nursing home once his or her or your funds are no longer available to pay for care. This can be emotionally devastating to the patient.)

Are these matters set out clearly in the written contract?

KNOW WHAT TO DO IF THERE IS A PROBLEM:
It's never any fun to have a dispute, but imagine if you were an infirm person who is confined to a nursing home and had to endure the horror of having a dispute with those responsible for your care. Imagine the fear you would have of confronting those responsible for your comfort and health and, perhaps, even your very life.   Under these conditions it is not right to expect the patient to have to fend for themselves. Someone from the family or a friend should be appointed as an informal patient advocate to communicate with the patient and intercede on his or her behalf when necessary (and, of course, spread compliments to the staff and administration when warranted). If no family member can or will undertake the responsiblity, hire a private geriatric care manager to do the job for you.
Here are some tips to help you in the event you become unhappy with your loved one's care:

Talk privately to the person involved in the problem: Before calling in the "big guns," such as the director of nursing, have a private chat with the person with whom your loved one has a dispute. You might be surprised that there are two sides to the controversy and how receptive he or she can be in trying to alleviate the problem. Such chats can keep molehills from becoming mountains.

Take the matter to the top: If talking in private doesn't help, call in either the director of nursing of the facility or the administrator or both. Remember, you are the source of the nursing home's business and most administrators know it and are likely to respond constructively to the problems you bring to their attention.

Call in the State Ombudsman: Each state has an office of nursing home ombudsman whose job it is to mediate problems that may arise between nursing homes and those they serve which cannot be solved by the parties themselves. The men and women who serve as ombudsmen are specially trained for the job and can usually pour oil on troubled waters. Contact your local chapter of the AARP or your local aging agency for the address and phone number.

Report the home to the authorities: If the problem is very serious, such as elder abuse, patient neglect or unsanitary facilities, report the home to the state health department and the state licensing authorities.

Avoid problems in the first place: The best way to solve problems is to identify potentially troublesome areas and deal with them before they become problems. This is done best by visiting often and ensuring that your loved one is receiving quality care. (For example, the existence of bedsores might indicate that a bedridden patient is not being turned often enough.) It is also a very good idea to humanize the patient in the staff's mind. In this regard, one nursing home I know has a picture of the patient taken in better times with a small list of accomplishments listed on the patient's door which reminds everyone that this now enfeebled and dependent person was once a vital and productive member of society and, as such, deserves respect and gentle loving care.

SPECIAL CONSIDERATIONS FOR ALZHEIMER'S CAREGIVERS

Alzheimer's disease deserves special mention because of its prevalence and because of the depth of care its victims require. This incurable disease begins its destruction of its victims initially with the degeneration of the brain's memory and ending with the inability of the body to maintain its own existence.

Because things can only go from bad to worse with Alzheimer's, caregivers must usually give of themselves beyond the call of duty. To put it bluntly, the job of caregiver is equivalent to combat duty. Here are some suggesstions to assist in that difficult assignment:

Families should join the Alzheimer's and Related Disease Association. Not only will this fine organization's in-depth educational resources be available to you, but perhaps more importantly there will also be an abundance of peer support from the families of other victims at your beck and call. To find your nearest chapter of ADRDA, call 800-621-0379 or in Illinois, 800-572-0379.

—If you are caring for your Alzheimer's victim at home, make a point of supervising their eating since sufferers have a strong tendency to forget or refuse to eat.

Obtain legal and financial planning. If they live long enough, every Alzheimer's victim will ultimately be rendered completely helpless by this disease. The cost of maintaining a decent level of care for victims, whether at home or in a nursing facility, is absolutely enormous and Medicaid does not kick in until the victim is virtually destitute. Lawyers who specialize in elder law and financial planners can help salvage as much of the family assets as possible, such as dividing the assets of husband and wife. Contact your local chapter of the ADRDA for more information. You may also want to obtain some estate planning of your own in the event something unfortunate should happen to you.

When the patient loses the ability to communicate with words that does not mean that he or she does not understand that they are loved. Continue to hug and kiss and stroke your loved one even if they are unable to respond.

Alzheimer's patients have a strong desire to wander. If you have one at home, he or she must not be left unattended. Daily exercise can limit this tendency. If you decide the time has come for a nursing home, be sure the home is able to cater to this tendency. There are homes that resort to tieing the patients in wheelchairs. Get an identification bracelet so that the patient can be identified should he or she wander and get lost.

Many Alzheimer's patients undergo personality changes such as suspiciousness, agitation and depression. The ADRDA can teach you methods of coping with this disturbing process of the disease.

And finally, once again, take care of yourself! Do only what you can do. Be sure that you receive enough respite so that you can maximize your own enjoyment of life. If you get in trouble, reach out for help. Many family support groups have 24-hour phone availability. In short, keep the stress that comes with being an Alzheimer's caregiver to a minimum. After all, the last thing you or your Alzheimer's patient needs is for you to have a heart attack or stroke.

A FINAL COMMENT

When I set out to write this book, I feared that the research and writing might be a depressing experience. After all, my subject was old age which has been advertised as a time of loss of physical prowess, of friends and loved ones and eventually, of life itself.

Well, I am happy to say that I have not come away from this writing feeling depressed at all. To the contrary, my innate optimism has only been reinforced. I have been privileged to communicate with men and women of tremendous energy and skill from all around the country who dedicate themselves to helping seniors enjoy a quality of life that has heretofore been unknown. I have witnessed the families of Alzheimer's victims gathered in a nursing home, loving their stricken relatives deeply and movingly, despite the fact that their love could not physically be given back in return. I have talked with eighty-year old lovers at a senior center who laughingly told me that they had their children's permission to, as they put it, "kick the can around one more time." In short, I have found that we truly are a nation of heroes.

I do not leave this enterprise depressed. I leave it greatly encouraged. Despite the problems, of which there remain many, life in the golden years can truly be a golden experience. That is not to say it doesn't take effort. It most certainly does. But that effort will reap the reward. And, as the immortal Ira Gershwin once asked, "Who could ask for anything more?"

■

SUPPLEMENT—U.S.A.

The following are the addresses and phone numbers of both state and territorial agencies and commissions on aging.

ALABAMA

Commission on Aging
136 Catoma Street, 2nd floor
Montgomery, Alabama 36130
(205) 261-5743

ALASKA

Older Alaskans Commission
Department of Administration
Pouch C-Mail Station 0209
Juneau, Alaska 99811-0209
(907) 465-3250

ARIZONA

Aging and Adult Administration
Department of Economic Security
1400 West Washington Street
Phoenix, Arizona 85007
(602) 255-3596

ARKANSAS

Division of Aging
   and Adult Services
Arkansas Department of
   Human Services
Donaghey Building, Suite 1417
7th and Main Streets
Little Rock, Arkansas 72201
(501) 682-2441

CALIFORNIA

Department of Aging
1600 K Street
Sacramento, California 95814
(916) 322-5290

COLORADO

Aging and Adult Service
Department of Social Services
1575 Sherman Street, 10th floor
Denver, Colorado 80203-1714
(303) 866-5905

CONNECTICUT

Department on Aging
175 Main Street
Hartford, Connecticut 06106
(203) 566-3238

DELAWARE

Division on Aging
Department of Health
   and Social Services
1901 North DuPont Highway
New Castle, Delaware 19720
(302) 421-6791

DISTRICT OF COLUMBIA

Office on Aging
1424 K. St. N.W., 2nd floor
Washington, D.C. 20005
(202) 724-5626

FLORIDA

Program Office of Aging
   and Adult Services
Department of Health and
   Rehabilitation Services
1317 Winewood Boulevard
Tallahassee, Florida 32301
(904) 488-8922

GEORGIA

Office of Aging
878 Peachtree Street, N.E.
Room 632
Atlanta, Georgia 30309
(404) 894-5333

GUAM

Division of Senior Citizens
Department of Public Health
  & Social Services
Government of Guam
Post Office Box 2816
Agana, Guam 96910

HAWAII

Executive Office of Aging
Office of the Govenor
335 Merchant St.
Room 241
Honolulu, Hawaii 96813
(808) 548-2593

IDAHO

Office on Aging
Room 114—Statehouse
Boise, Idaho 83720
(208) 334-3833

ILLINOIS

Department on Aging
421 East Capitol Avenue
Springfield, Illinois 62701
(217) 785-2870

INDIANA

Department of Human Services
251 North Illinois Street
P.O. Box 7083
Indianapolis, Indiana 46207-7083
(317) 232-1139

IOWA

Department of
  Elder Affairs
Suite 236, Jewett Building
914 Grand Avenue
Des Moines, Iowa 50319
(515) 281-5187

KANSAS

Department on Aging
610 West Tenth
Topeka, Kansas 66612
(913) 296-4986

KENTUCKY

Division for Aging Services
Cabinet for Human Resources
CHR Building, 6th floor
275 East Main Street
Frankfort, Kentucky 40601
(502) 564-6930

LOUISIANA

Office of Elderly Affairs
P.O. Box 80374
Baton Rouge, Louisiana 70898
(504) 925-1700

MAINE

Bureau of Maine's Elderly
Department of Human Services
State House—Station #11
Augusta, Maine 04333
(207) 289-2561

MARYLAND

Office of Aging
State Office Building
301 West Preston Street Rm. 1004
Baltimore, Maryland 21201
(301) 225-1100

MASSACHUSETTS

Executive Office of Elder Affairs
38 Chauncy Street
Boston, Massachusetts 02111
(617) 727-7750

MICHIGAN

Office of Services to the Aging
P.O. Box 30026
Lansing, Michigan 48909
(517) 373-8230

MINNESOTA

Board on Aging
Metro Square building, Room 204
Seventh and Robert Streets
St. Paul, Minnesota 55101
(612) 296-2770

MISSISSIPPI

Council on Aging
301 West Pearl Street
Jackson, Mississippi 39203-3092
(601) 949-2070

MISSOURI

Division on Aging
Department of Social Services
P.O. Box 1337
2701 West Main Street
Jefferson City, Missouri 65102
(314) 751-3082

MONTANA

Community Services Division
P.O. Box 4210
Helena, Montana 59604
(406) 444-3865

NEBRASKA

Department on Aging
P.O. Box 95044
301 Centennial Mall-South
Lincoln, Nebraska 68509
(402) 471-2306

NEVADA

Division for Aging Services
Department of Human Resourses
505 East King Street
Kinkead Building, Room 101
Carson City, Nevada 89710
(702) 885-4210

NEW HAMPSHIRE

Division of Elderly
& Adult Services
6 Hazen Drive
Concord, New Hampshire
03301-6501
(603) 271-4680

NEW JERSEY

Division on Aging
Department of Community Affairs
CN807
South Broad and Front Streets
Trenton, New Jersey 08625-0807
(609) 292-4833

NEW MEXICO

State Agency on Aging
224 East Palace Avenue, 4th Floor
La Villa Rivera Building
Santa Fe, New Mexico 87501
(505) 827-7640

NEW YORK

Office for the Aging
New York State Plaza
Agency Building #2
Albany, New York 12223
(518) 474-4425

NORTH CAROLINA

Assistant Secretary
Division of Aging
1985 Umstead Dr. Kirby Bldg.
Raleigh, North Carolina 27603
(919) 733-3983

NORTH DAKOTA

Aging Services
Department of Human Services
State Capitol Building
Bismarck, North Dakota 58505
(701) 224-2577

NORTHERN MARIANA ISLANDS

Office of Aging
Department of Community
  and Cultural Affairs
Civic Center—Susupe
Saipan
Northern Mariana Islands 96950
Tel. Nos. 9411 or 9732

OHIO

Department of Aging
50 West Broad Street, 9th floor
Columbus, Ohio 43266-0501
(614) 466-5500

OKLAHOMA

Special Unit on Aging
Department of Human Services
P.O. Box 25352
Oklahoma City, Oklahoma 73125
(405) 521-2281

OREGON

Senior Services Division
313 Public Service Building
Salem, Oregon 97310
(503) 378-4728

PENNSYLVANIA

Department of Aging
231 State Street
Harrisburg, Pennsylvania
17101-1195
(717) 783-1550

PUERTO RICO

Gericulture Commission
Department of Social Services
P.O. Box 11398
Santurce, Puerto Rico 00910
(809) 721-4010

RHODE ISLAND

Department of Elderly Affairs
79 Washington Street
Providence, Rhode Island 02903
(401) 277-2858

(AMERICAN) SAMOA

Territorial Administration
  on Aging
Office of the Governor
Pago Pago, American Samoa 96799
011 (684) 633-1252

SOUTH CAROLINA

Commission on Aging
Suite B-500
400 Arbor Lake Drive
Columbia, South Carolina 29223
(803) 735-0210

SOUTH DAKOTA

Office of Adult Services
   and Aging
700 North Illinois Street
Kneip Building
Pierre, South Dakota 57501
(605) 773-3656

TENNESSEE

Commission on Aging
Suite 201
706 Church Street
Nashville, Tennessee 37219-5573
(615) 741-2056

TEXAS

Department on Aging
P.O. Box 12786
Capitol Station
1949 IH 35,
South Austin, Texas 78741-3702
(512) 444-2727

TRUST TERRITORY
OF THE PACIFIC

Office of Elderly Programs
Community Development Division
Government of TTPI
Saipan, Mariana Islands 96950
Tel. Nos. 9335 or 9336

UTAH

Division of Aging
   and Adult Services
Department of Social Services
120 North, 200 West
Box 45500
Salt Lake City, Utah 84145-0500
(801) 538-3910

VERMONT

Office on Aging
103 South Main Street
Waterbury, Vermont 05676
(802) 241-2400

VIRGINIA

Department for the Aging
James Monroe Bldg., 18th Floor
101 North 14th Street
Richmond, Virginia 23219
(804) 225-2271

VIRGIN ISLANDS

Commission on Aging
6F Havensight Mall
Charlotte Amalie
St. Thomas, Virgin Islands 00801
(809) 774-5884

WASHINGTON

Aging and Adult
   Services Administration
Department of Social
   and Health Services
OB-44A
Olympia, Washington 98504
(206) 586-3768

WEST VIRGINIA

Commission on Aging
Holly Grove, State Capitol
Charleston, West Virginia 25305
(304) 348-3317

WISCONSIN

Bureau of Aging
Division of Community Services
One West Wilson Street Room 480
Madison, Wisconsin 53702
(608) 266-2536

WYOMING

Commission on Aging
Hathaway Building, Room 139
Cheyenne, Wyoming 82002-0710
(307) 777-7986

SUPPLEMENT-CANADA

The following are the addresses and phone numbers of both national and provincial agencies and commissions on aging.

NATIONAL

Department of National Health
  & Welfare
Income Security Programs Branch
Brooke Claxton Bldg.
Tunney's Pasture
Ottawa, ON K1A OL4
(613/957-1968) (TLX 053-3270)

National Advisory
  Council on Aging
Jeanne Mance Bldg. #1044
Ottawa ON K1A 0K9
(613/957-1968)

Canada Mtge. & Housing Corp.
Montreal Rd.
Ottawa ON K1A 0P7
(613/748-2600) (TLX 053-3674)

ALBERTA

Senior Citizen's Secretariat
10030 107 St.
Edmonton, AB T5J 3E4
(403/427-7876)

BRITISH COLUMBIA

GAIN for Seniors
Box 2500
Victoria, BC V8W 3A1
(604/387-4331)

Services to Seniors
Ministry of Social Services
  & Housing
Parliament Bldgs.
Victoria, BC V8V 1X4
(604/387-4331)

MANITOBA

55 Plus-A Manitoba Income
  Supplement
Manitoba Employment Services
  & Economic Security
330 Portage Ave. #500
Winnipeg, MB R3C 4B1
(204/945-2686)

NEW BRUNSWICK
Community Services Division
Department of Health
  & Community Services
Box 5000
Fredericton, NB E3B 1E6
(506/453-2181) (TLX 014-46230)
(TWX 610-233-4492)

NEWFOUNDLAND
Services to Senior Citizens
Department of Health
Confederation Bldg.
Box 4750
St. John's, NF A1C 5T7
(709/576-3554)

NOVA SCOTIA
Senior Citizens Secretariat
Box 2065
Halifax, NS B3J 2Z1
(902/424-6322)

Director of Family Benefits
Department of Social Services
Box 696
Halifax, NS B3J 2T7
(902/424-4262)

ONTARIO
Ministry of Community
  & Social Services
Operational Support Branch
Seniors & Family Support
700 Bay St.
Toronto, ON M7A 1E9
(416/965-8067) (TLX 06-23410)

Guaranteed Income
  & Tax Credit Branch
Ministry of Revenue
33 King St.
W. Oshawa, ON L1H 8H5
(416/433-6941)

Office for Senior Citizens' Affairs
76 College St., 6th floor
Queen's Park
Toronto, ON M7A 1N3
(416/965-5106)

Ontario Advisory Council
  on Senior Citizens
700 Bay St. #203
Toronto, ON M5G 1Z5
(416/965-2324)

PRINCE EDWARD ISLAND
Director
Aging & Extended Care Division
Department of Health
  & Social Services
Box 2000
Charlottetown, PE C1A 7N8
(902/892-5471) (TLX 014-44154)

QUEBEC
Ministere de la Sante
  et des Services Sociaux
Service de la documentation
1005, Chemin Ste-Foy, r.c.
Quebec, QC G1S 4N4
(418/643-7167) (TLX 051-3967)

SASKATCHEWAN
Seniors Bureau
Dept. of Human Resources,
Labour & Employment
2151 Scarth St.
Regina, SK S4P 3V7
(306/787-3182)

INDEX